#12

Celebrating the

100th Anniversary of
John Carter of Mars,
Tarzan of the Apes

and the worlds of

Edgar Rice Burroughs

Edited and compiled by Tom Roberts

2012
Normal, IL

The publisher wishes to thank the following individuals for additional contributions made to this volume: Doug Ellis, Gene Christie, John Locke, and Anthony Tollin.

ISBN 13 978-1-884449-29-1

Editing, book layout and design: Tom Roberts.
Proofreading: Doug Ellis.

Cover art by Stockton Mulford.

Black Dog Books, 1115 Pine Meadows Ct., Normal, IL 61761-5432.
www.blackdogbooks.net / info@blackdogbooks.net

Articles

Letters to ERB

Newly Discovered Writings

Special Fiction Section

Art Focus

Award Recognition

Filmfest Focus

Edgar Rice Burroughs, 1934.

EDGAR RICE BURROUGHS

Entertainment Is Fiction's Purpose

To frame an article on writing that will "be instructive and of real value to writers" requires something that I do not possess—a conscious knowledge of the technique of story writing. The best that I can do, therefore, is to discuss frankly my own methods, which will be utterly valueless to professional writers and of doubtful value to anyone else.

I find that a considerable part of my work in writing fiction has nothing whatsoever to do with fiction. It is based upon the belief that highly imaginative fiction, such as I write, demands the retention of a youthful and elastic mind, to achieve which one of my principal aims in life is to keep my body physically fit and my mind responsive to a diversity of simple stimuli.

For me, temperance is essential to good work. Simple amusements are the most desirable, and so far I have successfully avoided the acquisition of any sort of a hobby.

I understand that many men consider the acquisition of a hobby as absolutely essential to perfect mental contentment and consequent nerve rest and relaxation. My own observation leads me to believe that a single hobby is too narrowing an influence for a fiction writer and I should rather suggest the greater value of an interest in many things. I find it is better to have a little knowledge of many things than an expert knowledge of one, and the reason for this is obvious if you will consider the plight of the fiction writer, to reduce the example to an absurdity, whose hobby is the collection of postage stamps. It is necessary to give a great deal of time and thought to philately if one is to become expert in it, as I know by experience. Practically all of one's leisure time might be entertainingly devoted to his stamp collection, yet how seldom could this knowledge be used during the course of a writer's lifetime in the production of fiction?

> "I have no illusions of the literary value of my books, but I have the satisfaction of knowing that I gave my readers the best that my ability permitted." —ERB

The fiction writer should read most anything but fiction. He should be able to find entertainment in every form of sport, whether he is able to take an active part in it or not. He should enjoy a variety of games and other activities that keep his mind young and supple.

Please remember that I am speaking only of writers of highly imaginative

reprinted from *Writers Digest*, June 1930

fiction; concerning the others I know nothing. But the fiction writer to whom I refer should be what my two sons call monkey-minded—that is, have the tendency to caper erratically through the forest of human knowledge, swinging from tree to tree, tasting the fruits of many.

There is one thing that I would constantly impress upon the young writer—and possibly with greater reason upon the established writer—that he should not take either himself or his work too seriously. Except for purposes of entertainment, I consider fiction, like drama, an absolute unessential. I would not look to any fiction writer, living or dead, for guidance upon any subject, and, therefore, if he does not entertain, he is a total loss.

Every possible advantageous function of fiction may be found in history or biography, but for pure entertainment and mental relaxation nothing can take the place of fiction and drama, with the advantages all on the side of fiction since it may be had economically and in comfort at home.

The man who takes himself and his work too seriously is certain to attempt something for which he is not fitted, with the result that he soon loses whatever following he may have created, or if he is a beginner, he never achieves any such following.

In fiction the reader has a right to expect entertainment and relaxation. If obscenities entertain him he can always find fiction that will fulfill his requirements. If he wishes to be frightened or thrilled or soothed, he will find writers for his every mood, but you may rest assured that he does not wish to be instructed. He does not wish to have to think, and as fully ninety percent of the people in the world are not equipped with anything wherewith to think intelligently, the fiction writer who wishes to be a success should leave teaching to qualified teachers and attend strictly to his business of entertaining.

I have been writing for nineteen years and I have been successful probably because I have always realized that I knew nothing about writing and have merely tried to tell an interesting story entertainingly. But there is another reason for the continued success of my books which I should like to impress upon younger writers. From the beginning I have adhered to a policy of ordinary business honesty that was instilled into me by my father. My first stories were the best stories that I could write and every story that I have written since has been the very best story that I could write. I have felt that it was a duty to those people who bought my books that I should give them the very best within me. I have no illusions as to the literary value of what I did give them, but I have the satisfaction of knowing that I gave them the best that my ability permitted.

The result of this policy has been the continued interest of my earliest readers in all my subsequent novels. Unquestionably they have not liked them all equally well, but I think not many of them have ever been keenly disappointed.

It is the reading public that either makes or breaks you, and if you are fortunate enough to have one successful book redouble your efforts to write a better one the next.

* * * * *

This article is intended for people who are writing or hope to write for their livelihood and to such it is probably unnecessary to state that publicity is essential to success, no matter how much one may shrink from it—or pretend to shrink from it. But there is a matter of professional ethics involved, as well as ordinary good taste, which I believe should always be in the mind of every writer. I have no patience whatsoever with the man who does a rude, unkindly or discourteous thing for the purpose of obtaining publicity. I have no patience with a professional writer who begs or buys publicity; nor with the writer who makes a fool of himself in order to obtain it.

It is perfectly proper for your publishers to buy publicity for you. That is their business, not yours. And it is perfectly proper for you, at their request, to furnish them with any material that they may require for this purpose, but outside of this I consider it unethical for a writer to seek publicity.

I have had close personal and business relations with newspapermen all over the United States, both publishers and editors, numbering among them many good friends, yet I have never, either directly or indirectly, asked or expected any personal publicity from them; nor have I ever paid for any publicity. Perhaps I carry this principle to an extreme, since I will not permit my name to be inserted in any directory or encyclopedia which solicits either money or subscriptions as a price for representation in their work from any one appearing in it.

If this article leaves any thought with you, I hope it is that the profession of fiction writing should be carried on upon a high plane of business integrity and professional ethics without any vain and silly illusions as to the importance of fiction outside of the sphere of entertainment.

· · · · ·

The Beasts of Tarzan

By Edgar Rice Burroughs

More thrilling adventures of Tarzan, the marvelous ape-man.

AT ALL BOOKSTORES
A. C. McClurg & Co., Pubs.

1916 newspaper advertisement

Discover New Thrills from Black Dog Books

Need More Excitement?

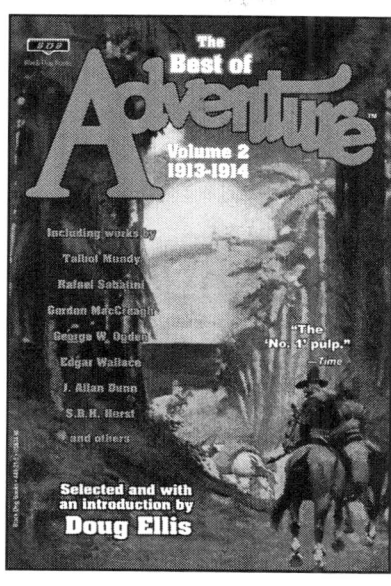

THE BEST OF ADVENTURE
Vol, 2—1913-1914
396 pp. / $34.95
The follow-up to our highly acclaimed *Best of Adventure, Vol.1*, this collection brings together 19 of the best tales that appeared in *Adventure,* including rarely or never-before reprinted works by Talbot Mundy, Rafael Sabatini, Edgar Wallace, H.D. Couzens, J. Allan Dunn, George Washington Ogden, Stephen Chalmers and others.
With an introduction by Doug Ellis.

WEB OF THE SUN
T.S. STRIBLING
205 pp. / $19.95
Journey to South America to uncover two strange mysteries by Pulitzer Prize Winner T.S. Stribling. With an introduction by Richard A. Moore.

EMPIRE OF THE DEVIL
FREDERICK NEBEL
290 pp. / $24.95
Hunt lost treasure in Borneo, pursue a cursed gem in India, battle a secret society in the Orient, unravel a mystery at sea, flee from headhunters and more in these 8 thrilling tales.

Black Dog Books
www.blackdogbooks.net
info@blackdogbooks.net

The Tarzan Theme

A titled English Lord and his lady leave England on government business for Africa. They arrive safely and journey to the heart of that savage Continent to do their business, which consists in part of rearing their small male son. Before the babe can do more than toddle, his father and mother are killed by the jungle apes. A female ape whose offspring was just killed adopts the little white babe, who is reared to giant manhood by the apes, who call him Tarzan, meaning white skin.

From this bare plot Edgar Rice Burroughs has spun a thousand tales, not to speak of cartoon strips, scenarios, and radio continuities. Tarzan is the unashamed idol of a million small boys and the fond recollection of several more million adults. Tarzan, as we have previously remarked, has won his way into the consciousness of the nation, if not, as Mr. Burroughs notes, into the dictionary.

Someone is always taking the joy out of life. For twenty years I proceed blissfully writing stories to keep the wolf from my door and to cause other people to forget for an hour or two the wolves at their doors, and then up pops the editor of *Writer's Digest* and asks me for an article on the Tarzan theme.

Frankly, there ain't no sich animal; or if there is I didn't know it.

Breathlessly, I flew to Mr. Webster, determined to create a Tarzan theme with his assistance; but I was disappointed in somehow not finding Tarzan in the dictionary. But I did find "theme." Webster calls it: "A subject or topic on which a person writes or speaks; a proposition for discussion or argument; a text."

That definition simplified my task for under this definition the Tarzan theme consists of one word—Tarzan.

This is a helpful solution because it is easy and right now I am as busy as the one-armed paper hanger with the hives. I have to write two novels a year in addition to other writing; I am publishing my own books now, two a year, which entails a tremendous amount of detail; then there are seven newspaper strips a week in addition to motion pictures and radio. Being in the real estate business as a sideline adds to my labors, though not greatly for the past two years, as any realtor will tell you, unless paying taxes comes under the head of labor.

On top of all this, I have recently acquired by foreclosure a championship eighteen-hole golf course at Tarzana, California, which I have partially opened to the public for tournament play.

A few days ago a good natured columnist commented on my activities in the New York *Evening Telegram* as follows:

reprinted from *Writers Digest,* June 1932

"Edgar Rice Burroughs is marketing his book, *Jungle Girl,* from his home in Tarzana, California. Mr. Burroughs is the nation's sixth largest industry, now that steel and railroads are slowing up."

Had he known about the golf course, I think he might have moved me up.

There is, however, one great advantage in all these activities. I have always required a great deal of exercise, but the amount that I must now take is considerably lessened by the fact that all these things, especially the real estate business, make me sweat without any other effort.

Getting back to the theme—"a proposition for discussion or argument," says Mr. Webster. The Tarzan stories are a means for avoiding discussion or argument, so that definition is out, and there only remains the last, "a text." As this connotes sermonizing we shall have to hit it on the head, which leaves me nothing at all to write about on the Tarzan theme.

Tarzan does not preach; he has no lesson to impart, no propaganda to disseminate. Yet, perhaps unconsciously, while seeking merely to entertain I have injected something of my own admiration for certain fine human qualities into these stories of the ape-man.

It is difficult and even impossible for me to take these Tarzan stories seriously, and I hope that no one else will ever take them seriously. If they serve any important purpose it is to take their readers out of the realm of serious things and give them that mental relaxation which I believe to be as necessary as the physical relaxation of sleep—which makes a swell opening for some dyspeptic critic.

I recall that when I wrote the first Tarzan story twenty years ago I was mainly interested in playing with the idea of a contest between heredity and environment. For this purpose I selected an infant child of a race strongly marked by hereditary characteristics of the finer and nobler sort, and at an age at which he could not have been influenced by association with creatures of his own kind I threw him into an environment as diametrically opposite that to which he had been born as I might well conceive.

As I got into the story I realized that the logical result of this experiment must have been a creature that would have failed to inspire the sympathy of the ordinary reader, and that for fictional purposes I must give heredity some breaks that my judgment assured me the facts would not have warranted. And so Tarzan grew into a creature endowed only with the best characteristics of the human family from which he was descended and the best of those which mark the wild beasts that were his only associates from infancy until he had reached man's estate.

It has pleased me throughout the long series of Tarzanian exploits to draw comparisons between the manners of men and the manners of beasts and seldom to the advantage of men. Perhaps I hoped to shame men into being more like beasts in those respects in which the beasts excel men, and these are not few.

I wanted my readers to realize that man alone of all the creatures that inhabit the earth or the waters below or the air above takes life wantonly; he is the only creature that derives pleasure from inflicting pain on other creatures, even his own kind. Jealousy, greed, hate, spitefulness are more fully developed in man than in the lower orders. These are axiomatic truths that require no demonstration.

Even the lion is merciful when he makes his kill, though doubtless not intentionally so; and the psychology of terror aids the swift mercy of his destruction. Men who have been charged and mauled by lions, and lived to tell of the experience, felt neither fear nor pain during the experience.

In the quite reasonable event that this statement may arouse some skepticism, permit me to quote from that very splendid work on animals, *Mother Nature*, by William J. Long, a book that should be read by every adult and be required reading in every high school course in the land.

"There are other and more definite experiences from which to form a judgment, and of these the adventure of Livingston is the first to be considered, since he was probably the first to record the stupefying effects of a charging animal. The great missionary and explorer was once severely mauled by a lion, his flesh being torn in eleven places by the brute's claws, and his shoulder crushed by the more terrible fangs. Here is a condensation of the story, as recorded in *Missionary Travels and Research in South Africa*:

> Growling horribly close to my ear, the lion shook me as a terrier does a rat. The shock produced a stupor similar to that which seems to be felt by a mouse after the first shake of the cat. It caused a sort of dreaminess, in which there was no sense of pain nor feeling of terror.

> Compare this, then, with the methods of the present day gangster who cruelly tortures his victim before he kills him. The lion sought only to kill, not to inflict pain. Recall the methods of the Inquisition, and then search the records of man's experiences with lions, tigers, or any of the more formidable creatures of the wild for a parallel in studied cruelty.

Let me quote one more interesting instance given in Mr. Long's book:

We open at random to the experience of an English officer who, in 1895, was fearfully clawed and bitten by a lion, and who writes of the experience:

"Regarding my sensations during the time the attack upon me by the lion was in progress, I had no feeling of pain whatever, although there was a distinct feeling of being bitten; that is, I was perfectly conscious, independently of seeing the performance, that the lion was gnawing at me, but there was no pain. To show that the feeling, or rather want of it, was in no wise due to excessive terror I may mention that, whilst my thighs were being gnawed, I took two cartridges out of the breast pocket of my shirt and threw them to the Kaffir, who was hovering a few yards away, telling him to load my rifle."

Perhaps I am not wise in giving further publicity to these statements, since they must definitely take much of the thrill out of Tarzan stories by placing lion mauling in a category with interesting and pleasurable experiences.

In his latest novel, *Jungle Girl*, Mr. Burroughs starts off on another trail, but we can sense in its title that it is akin to the "Tarzan theme."

Jungle Girl. Edgar Rice Burroughs, 1932, First edition

Having demonstrated that the most savage animals in their most terrifying moods reveal qualities far less terrible than those possessed by man, let us see how association with these beasts combined with the hereditary instincts of a noble blood line to produce in Tarzan a character finer than either of the sources from which it derived.

Necessity required him to kill for food and in defense of his life, the example of his savage associates never suggested that pleasure might be found in killing, and the chivalry that was in his bloodstream prevented him imagining such pleasure in youth without such example. His viewpoint toward death was seemingly callous, but it was without cruelty.

His attitude toward women and other creatures weaker than he was partially the result of innate chivalry, partially the natural outcome of a feeling of superiority engendered both by knowledge of his mental or physical superiority to every creature that had come within his ken and by heredity, and partially by an indifference born of absolute clean-mindedness and perfection of health.

His appeal to an audience is so tremendous that it never ceases to be a source of astonishment to me. This appeal, I believe, is based upon an almost universal admiration of these two qualities and the natural inclination of every normal person to enjoy picturing himself as either heroic or beautiful or both. Linked to these is the constant urge to escape that is becoming stronger in all of us prisoners of civilization as civilization becomes more complex.

We wish to escape not alone the narrow confines of city streets for the freedom of the wilderness, but the restrictions of man made laws, and the inhibitions that society has placed upon us. We like to picture ourselves as roaming free, the lords of ourselves and of our world; in other words, we would each like to be Tarzan. At least I would; I admit it.

Unconsciously or consciously, we seek to emulate the creatures we admire. Doubtless there are many people trying to be like the late Theodore Roosevelt, or like Robert Millikan, or Jack Dempsey, or Doug Fairbanks because they greatly admire one of these characters. Fiction characters are just as real to most of us as are these celebrities of today or the past; d'Artagnan is as much flesh and blood as Napoleon. Perhaps the influence of d'Artagnan has had a finer influence upon the forming of character than has that of the great Corsican.

To indicate the force for good which a fiction character may exercise I can do no better than cite the testimony of Eddie Eagan, Amateur Heavyweight Champion of the World, whose very interesting series of articles appeared in the *Saturday Evening Post*. As a boy Eagan read the Frank Merriwell books, and his admiration for this fiction character shaped his future life. Among other achievements Merriwell became an athlete and a Yale man, and these became two of Eagan's ambitions. Although a poor boy, Eagan worked his way through an education, first in college in Denver, then through Yale, and finally Oxford; and he became one of the greatest athletes of our times.

Years ago, when I came to a realization of the hold that Tarzan had taken upon the imaginations of many people, I was glad that I had made of him the sort of character that I had; and since then I have been careful not to permit him to let his foot slip, no matter what the temptation. I must admit that at times this has been difficult when I have placed him in situations where I would not have been quite sure of my own footing, and it has also not been easy to keep him from being a Prue.

On the whole, however, I must have been more or less successful for all ages and both sexes continue to admire him; and he goes his bloody way scattering virtue and sudden death indiscriminately and in all directions.

He may not be a force for good; and if he entertains, that is all I care about; but I am sure that he is not a force for evil, which is something these days.

· · · · ·

1915 newspaper advertisement

J. Allen St. John

"First, I read over our manuscript for the pleasure it affords me
and to absorb the spirit of it. A second time to make notations of such
situations, as, in my opinion would lend themselves best to pictures. Then follow
the "layouts" without models. They in turn are trued up for size, enlarged, and
the models and other data brought into play for the finished drawings."
—St. John, writing to ERB

ROBERT WEINBERG

J. Allen St. John: A Short Biography

Born in Chicago, James Allen St. John (1872-May 27, 1957) was the grandson of Hilliard Hely, a well-known artist of the nineteenth century. Hely's daughter (St. John's mother) also wanted to be an artist and traveled to Paris when her son was only eight years old, taking the boy with her. The young child was allowed to wander at will through the Louvre and other major art museums of Europe, and he began to sketch and paint before he could read or write.

St. John returned to America and began his formal schooling. His father tried to make him a businessman and, when the artist was sixteen, bought him a partnership with an experienced businessman. St. John protested and finally was sent west to live on his uncle's ranch in California. On a trip to Los Angeles, he met Eugene Torrey, a western artist, and they became fast friends. St. John immediately decided to become an artist and spent time the next several years traveling throughout the West, drawing and painting.

St. John moved to the East Coast in the waning days of the nineteenth century, working as a portrait painter in the New York area and also doing landscapes and nature scenes. By then he was a well-regarded society artist.

St. John moved to Chicago in the early years of the twentieth century. The artist lived in his own private studio in his native city, in a three-story artist complex known as "The Tree Studio." The special building was designed specifically for artists and combined living quarters and studio space. Each residence had a large studio with a skylight. St. John's apartment was on the first floor and had a private garden with a fountain. He lived there with his wife, Ellen, until his death in 1957.

St. John worked as an illustrator for the numerous publishing companies in Chicago for nearly fifty years. The first book he illustrated, *The Face in the Pool,* was published in 1904. It was the first of many works he would illustrate for the A.C. McClurg company.

Along with a busy career as an illustrator, St. John worked as an instructor of painting and illustration at the Art Institute of Chicago for twenty years. He later joined the faculty of the American Academy of Art, where he served as professor of life drawing and illustration.

St. John's first artwork of importance in the science fiction field was done in 1916, when he illustrated the first hardcover edition of *The Beasts of Tarzan* by Edgar Rice Burroughs. The book featured more than thirty black-and-white il-

This article originally appeared in *A Biographical Dictionary of Science Fiction and Fantasy Artists* by Robert Weinberg, Greenwood Press, 1988, and is reprinted by permission of the author.

lustrations by St. John and a color jacket. He even did the lettering for the book, a tradition he was to continue for all of the Burroughs books he illustrated. In 1917 he was given the assignment of illustrating *The Son of Tarzan*. Again, the artist turned out more than thirty pen-and-ink illustrations, along with a color jacket and the lettering for the title page. When the A.C. McClurg company prepared to publish Burrough's third Mars novel, the art assignment was given to St. John, who was becoming known as the Burroughs artist. For *The Warlord of Mars*, he did a stunning oil painting for the jack-et. It was probably the finest illustration done for any Burrough's novel up to that time. When McClurg made plans to pub-lish the next Mars novel, *Thuvia, Maid of Mars*, St. John was again given the cover assignment along with a commission for ten full-page illustrations. He had then become the accepted Burroughs artist.

The Son of Tarzan. A.C. McClurg and Co., 1917. First edition.

Burroughs was not the only author for whom St. John did book illustrations, but he was definitely the most famous, and his name became closely linked with the Tarzan author. St. John continued do-ing work for Burroughs novels into the early 1930s, mostly for hardcover edi-tions, although he did a cover for *Blue-book* magazine as well, illustrating one of the later Tarzan novels. St. John also did jacket art for a number of other McClurg hardcover editions, including several sci-ence fiction novels by Ray Cummings.

St. John was an accomplished artist and did excellent work in all mediums. Most of his paintings were done in oils, but he also was adept in watercolors. His interior work was done in both pen and ink and in gouache. He also did interior art in pencil and charcoal crayon. He worked with large sizes, and many of his full-page wash paintings that were used as black-and-white illustrations in book form were twenty-two by thirty-two inches or larger. When St. John did the jacket painting for *Jungle Tales of Tarzan*, A.C. McClurg asked him to do a large paint-ing so that they could use it on a tour to sell the book. The painting, of an eagle carrying Tarzan away, was four by six feet.

In the early 1930s Edgar Rice Burroughs formed his own publishing com-pany to print his novels. Feeling that St. John charged too much for his art, Bur-roughs began using other artists, including some of his own relatives such as Studley Burroughs and John Coleman Burroughs. By 1936 the last of St. John's art for the Burroughs company appeared in hardcover. Losing his best client, St. John tried to get started in the comic strip field, producing a Sunday page based on the John Carter series. Nothing came from this attempt.

Living in Chicago, St. John was well known as an artist and art teacher. Looking for other assignments to make up for the loss of the Burroughs work, St. John found *Weird Tales* magazine being published in the city. He soon began doing covers for that magazine along with its sister publication, *Magic Carpet*. In late 1932 *Weird Tales* serialized "Buccaneers of Venus" by Otis Adelbert Kline, a fantasy novel very much in the Burroughs style. St. John was the obvious choice to illustrate the novel, and he did four covers for the serial.

Unfortunately, the artist soon found himself without assignments from the pulp. Margaret Brundage also began doing work for the same magazine in late 1932. Although St. John's paintings were much more fantastic than Brundage's, magazine editor Farnsworth Wright thought that

Jungle Tales of Tarzan. A.C. McClurg and Co., 1919. First edition.

sex sold better than fantastic monsters. Brundage was retained, and St. John was dropped from the covers. He later did a few *Weird Tales* cover paintings, but the magazine never became a steady source of income. An interesting sidelight of St. John's work for *Weird Tales* was that in doing cover illustrations for the pulp, he did his own lettering for the logo of the magazine. Even after they stopped using the artist for the covers, *Weird Tales* retained the cover logo style, and it became closely identified with the magazine.

In late 1940 Ray Palmer, editor of the Ziff-Davis science fiction magazines *Amazing Stories* and *Fantastic Adventures,* bought a series of novelettes from Edgar Rice Burroughs to run in those publications. Ziff-Davis was located in Chicago and the company tried to have local artists do the magazine illustrations. Palmer, a longtime science fiction collector, immediately contacted St. John, who illustrated the Burroughs novelettes and continued to work for the two science fiction magazines throughout the 1940s.

St. John also continued to teach in Chicago throughout the 1940s and early 1950s. He did a few more paintings for Chicago-based magazines, including *Fate* and *Other Worlds,* during this period, and he sold a number of his originals to collectors visiting his studios. He died in May 1957.

With the revival of interest in Burroughs's work in the 1960s, St. John's name once again became famous. His influence on the work of Roy Krenkel and Frank Frazetta was noted and appreciated by modern fantasy fans. A commemorative volume reproducing much of his art also helped boost his reputation. Among older collectors, St. John was already considered one of the greatest of all fantasy artists. With the new attention accorded him, he became equally well known among younger fans and artists. His originals, always scarce, became prime collectibles and have been sold for thousands of dollars, making his works among the most expensive of all fantasy illustrators.

J. Allen St. John—illustration for *The Son of Tarzan*, 1917.

J. Allen St. John—illustration for *Thuvia, Maid of Mars*, 1920.

Illustration for "Black Pirates of Barsoom" by Burroughs, *Amazing Stories,* June 1941.

Illustration for "War on Venus" by Burroughs, *Fantastic Adventures,* March 1942.

OLIVER POOLE

"Romance Isn't Dead"

(An interview with the author of Tarzan)

To get to Edgar Rice Burroughs' home, you head for the sea. You drive out along Hollywood Boulevard to Sunset and along Sunset toward Beverly Hills. Just before you get to Beverly you come to a stretch of new Georgian-fronted shop; and office buildings, with here and there a popular night club . . . a little white village known as "The Strip," not because it's any relation to Sally Rand (the fan dancer) but because it is literally a strip of road bordered by tiny smart shops and the swank new offices of important motion picture agents. I drove past art galleries, interior decorators, modistes, de luxe antiquarians, gay restaurants and gift shops (including Eddie Cantor's). Though it was January by the calendar the weather was as balmy as it is in June . . . it was one of those blue and gold, let's-be-happy days. Everything glittered in the sunlight, especially the white front of the famous "Trocadero" café (where the stars dine, and sometimes wine). There I swung about, crossed the boulevard and drove up into the hills through a newly opened section of bare brown land where the brand new Sunset-Plaza Apartments are located. These are the latest thing in the way of apartments . . . really a series of white houses joined together about a huge terrace.

It isn't at all the sort of a place in which you'd expect to find the author of the "Tarzan" books. I don't know exactly what I did expert unless it was a rustic house set in a bit of wild woodland and Mr. Burroughs swinging from the chandelier. Certainly not this spick and span up-to-dateness with nary a woodland in sight . . . only immaculate concrete tennis courts.

And he's a surprise, too . . . the man who created "Tarzan." He's decidedly a cosmopolitan, a gentleman author (they're rare as hen's teeth in these days of roughneck writers). He is tall, slim, and as carefully dressed as a picture in *Esquire*. He has a grand sense of humor, a genial manner and his wife calls him 'Ed.' He has the most soothing, the most bland voice I have ever listened to, and it told me interesting things about the writing of books and stories that sell.

"I think," he began, "that it is rather necessary these days, as it always has been, to create a lovable, or at least an interesting character around which to weave your story. That is, if you intend to continue writing and keep your public interested. And a main character with serial possibilities is a good idea. Remember, the public is growing more and more serial-minded. The radio is more or less responsible for this desire for serials. It has trained its listeners (who constitute the greater part of the American world) to grow curious about one certain character,

reprinted from *Writer's Markets and Methods,* March 1938

or set of characters. Take, for instance, Charlie McCarthy, Amos and Andy, "One Man's Family." The comic strip began it and the screen (with its early serials and its later Charlie Chan plays) helped.

"I believe, too, that the leading character or characters of a story should have a romantic setting or go through romantic adventures . . . mild or hair-raising ones . . . if you wish to hold your readers. But be the adventures mild or wild they should be romantic."

"But, Mr. Burroughs," I objected, "I thought the new trend was to pooh-pooh romance and go after the unadorned facts of life. I thought romance was supposed to be dead."

"Don't you ever believe it!" Mr. Burroughs answered hurriedly. "Romance *isn't* dead . . . never *was* dead . . . and *never will be dead* as long as man exists! We need it, so we will always demand it! What kind of fiction sells year after year, steadily and with no lessening of the public's interest? Romantic fiction . . . doesn't it?"

I nodded.

"That's why people continue to buy the Tarzan stories, why Tarzan's adventures continue to be popular as picture serials in the daily paper and as screen attractions. What else could it be?"

"Where," I asked curiously, "did you get the idea for Tarzan? Was he carefully planned or just an accidental thing?"

"Rather accidental. He was just a character that happened to catch the public's fancy. Interest in him grew until it astonished me. As a boy I loved the story of Romulus and Remus, who founded Rome, and I loved, too, the boy Mowgli in Kipling's 'Jungle Books.' I suppose Tarzan was the result of those early loves. Perhaps the fact that I lived in Chicago and yet hated cities and crowds of people made me write my first Tarzan story. . . . Tarzan was, in a sense, my escape from unpleasant reality. Perhaps that is the reason for his success with modern readers. Maybe he takes them, too, away from humdrum reality.

"Mrs. Burroughs calls me a low-brow. I guess I am, but then so are the most of us, aren't we? Perhaps that is another reason why Tarzan appeals to the mass of people rather than to a select few."

"It's more than that," I retorted. "And I object to the term low-brow applied to you. You are one of the few significant names in American letters today, and despite depressions and rumors of war you continue to sell. Maybe you're right . . . maybe romance is the best entertainment."

"Well, my sales dropped off considerably during the depression, as the sales of most books did, because few people had the price of a book but almost everyone had a radio and the radio offers excellent entertainment. Who knows but what future generations may cease reading books altogether and take for their mental amusement the screen, radio and television? It's a changing world."

I took this without blinking.

"That last remark of yours brings us to the subject of *Writers' Markets and Methods,*" I said. "We hope to arouse a wide interest in writers and writing . . .

we want to keep the author before the public eye. We want to build him up as a personality and thus awaken an interest in the things he writes. We want to make America author-conscious. We want books to continue . . . not to dwindle away. The writers seem to us to be the Forgotten People of today . . . forgotten as personalities."

Mr. Burroughs considered this carefully.

"You probably won't succeed," he said, "for the writer has become too nebulous a personality today . . . screen and radio stars have taken his place. This is because the stars' faces are kept constantly before the public. My face and the faces of other authors are not kept before the public . . . probably for the very good reason that we, as a rule, are not beautiful to look at. Today it is exteriors and externals that count, not ideas that come out of one's head."

"Just the same." I objected, "we intend to *plug* for the writer, for books, for bigger and better stories and to discover and praise style and fiction characters if they are worth praising. Literature is one of the arts . . . along with music, sculpture, architecture and painting. The arts are said to be the soul of a nation, aren't they? Without them we can have nothing but economic plans and political views. And in order that these arts exist we must create an appreciative circle for them, some group to support them and to maintain a high standard . . . and we are going to do our best toward creating this appreciative circle for the writers."

Mr. Burroughs eyes danced.

On the wall of the charming sitting room where we were chatting was an astonishingly good painting . . . a gorgeous bit of color.

"My boy is the artist," Mr. Burroughs told me proudly. He nodded toward a child's head and a painting of old Mexico on another wall. "He has an exhibition now at Robinson's. He illustrated my last book. I'm very proud of him."

I studied the paintings carefully . . . they held a certain sultry quality in their coloring that cried "Jungle!" It was much more believable to me that Edgar Rice Burrough's son should paint as he does than that Mr. Burroughs should be a thorough-going cosmopolite, that he should live far from any wood in an ultra-modern apartment, and that there should be no literary props around . . . just his son's paintings and Mrs. Burroughs' grand piano standing in the sunlight of a great bay-window and bowls of garden flowers everywhere. Somehow I expected that the man who writes of jungle apes, of stone-age men, of life on Mars and Venus would be unconventional. The contrast between the picture in my mind and reality was dramatic, as contrasts always are. Probably that's why I got such a "kick" out of the interview . . . a "kick" which I have tried to pass on to you.

• • • • •

Edgar Rice Burroughs, Inc.

It was only an account of one of Los Angeles' many auto collisions, but it made the natives reading it look twice to make sure. Just a bumper-locking with no one hurt; but when the *News* reported that one of the drivers "leaped out of his car without a bellow," many readers felt they had picked up a newspaper 20 years old. The bellowless driver was Edgar Rice Burroughs.

For most of us, Tarzan of the Apes, like Paul Bunyan, is a part of folk literature, and the guy who first thought him up couldn't still be around. Well, Burroughs is—he'll be 74 this year, and he isn't happy about it. Even though none of his writing is autobiographic in so many words, Burroughs has always identified himself with his superman heroes.

In *Tarzan and the Foreign Legion*, the 23rd of that series, published in 1947, the ape-man revealed he had achieved a twice-assured eternal youth, once from a grateful witch doctor and once from a compound distilled from glands of young girls. In *The Chessmen of Mars*, the fifth of *that* series, published in 1922, John Carter said, "I am a very old man. I do not know how old I am but I never age and I love life and the vigor of youth." Edgar Rice Burroughs is reluctant to give up the identification. "I'm afraid I don't know how to grow old gracefully," he complained to a visitor recently. "You see, I never expected to grow old."

At 55, when many men want nothing more violent than to fish and philosophize on their $150-a-month insurance money, Burroughs took up flying; at 59 he married an actress, Florence Gilbert Dearholt, 29 years his junior; at 66 he joined the Businessmen's Training Corps of Honolulu; and at 67 he became the country's oldest war correspondent, covering the Pacific for the UP on an oiler named *Cahaba*. From '42 to '45, Burroughs lived in some degree the adventurous kind of life he had hitherto only written about.

Let one of the fellows he met in the islands pop in for a visit and the talk goes like this: "Remember the night the kamikaze hit the oiler ahead of us?" A look of nostalgia comes into Burroughs' now-puffy eyes. "How about the sniper

reprinted from *Writers Digest*, August 1949

who tried to pick you off on Zamma Shima?" "Sniper!" Burroughs snorts. "He couldn't hit a jeep with five passengers in it!" "Yeah, your friend Landon was a whole lot more dangerous than any Jap. Remember the crackup when you had to drop out of the tail-hatch?" "I asked for it," says Burroughs wistfully. "Darned nice of the chap to take me on the mission. I always wanted to get over Tokyo with the bombs." It was in the service during his 70th year that Burroughs, first became aware there was such a thing as old age.

Until he did, come hell or high water, Burroughs continued to turn out two or three books a year, making more money than any other writer who ever wiggled pen across paper. Fifty-seven of Burroughs' books have appeared in more than 50 languages and dialects, selling more than 35,000,000 copies, with Burroughs' share of the cash receipts running perhaps to $5,000,000. Twenty-five Tarzan movies have grossed over $30,000,000. With his current deal, Burroughs receives $200,000 a picture just for the use of the character, his total share to date running at least $3,000,000. The Tarzan comic strip appears in 291 U.S. newspapers, paying Burroughs an annual royalty of between $50,000 and $65,000.

For years, there was a Tarzan radio show; *Tarzan El Indomito* is still running on the air in South America, a sort of Spanish soap opera sponsored by Palmolive Peet. Besides, there are the Tarzan comic books, and, at one time, there were Tarzan trapezes, jungle suits, masks, penknives, rubber daggers, holsters, chewing gum, jawbreakers, sweaters, schoolbags, pencils, crayons, paint books, soaps, breads, ice cream cups, mechanical toys, balloons, statuettes, games, and other such goods, each leased at so much per—in other words, Tarzan was the Shmoo of the '20s. The only comment Burroughs will make about the grand money total is: "It proves a rolling stone can gather some moss."

If you would like to start off by being a rolling stone, Burroughs is a fine model. The son of a well-to-do battery manufacturer, Edgar Rice went from a private Chicago school to a military academy. When he flunked the West Point entrance exams and failed to obtain commissions in the Chinese and Nicaraguan armies, he enlisted in the United States 7th Cavalry, stationed in Arizona. Bored and underage, he secured a discharge and went to Idaho to herd cattle on his brother's ranch, to Oregon to dredge for gold, to Utah to take a job as a railroad yard cop.

In 1900, while working in his father's electric battery plant at $15 a week, he married Emma Centennia Hulbert. He soon tired of batteries and went back to Idaho, going into the stationery store business. He got back to Chicago by auctioning off his furniture. Hating selling, he became, in succession, a salesman of light bulbs, candy, and Stoddard's Travel Lectures. "I only read enough of the lectures to talk about them," he says of his sales psychology. "I'd get my foot in the door and say in one breath, 'Mr. Stoddard asked me to call on you.' The uppers of my shoes wore out trying to keep doors open."

He was a Sears Roebuck manager when his daughter Joan was born, failed in a combination sales course-aluminum pot business of his own at the time his son Hulbert was born and had to pawn his wife's jewelry to keep the family eating. To keep from going crazy with insomnia nights, he used to imagine himself flying through space to a less cruel world like Mars or swinging through the friendly jungle, top man—nay, superman—of both.

Burroughs was so devoid of hope that at 35, while peddling a lead-pencil sharpener, he began writing stories nights and Sundays. "I considered all fiction silly," he confesses, "and never read it, but I was desperate." Halfway through his first story, Burroughs had doubts that anyone else would want to read it, so he sent what he had to *All-Story* magazine. Editor Thomas Newell Metcalf wrote back, "Finish it," which Burroughs did at once. With his aptitude for the self-singing name, he called the story *Dejah Thoris, Princess of Mars*, but Metcalf published it as *Under the Moon of Mars*. Later it was issued as Burroughs' fifth book, *A Princess of Mars*.

In 1912, Burroughs dropped the self-depreciating pseudonym, Normal Bean (average brain) he had been using, and began his most famous opus, basing it on his wishful projection of five years before. "I started my thoughts on the legend of Romulus and Remus who had been suckled by a wolf and founded Rome," he explains, "but in the jungle I had my little Lord Greystoke suckled by an ape."

In 1913, when his third child and later illustrator, John, was born, and Street & Smith paid him $1000 for *The Return of Tarzan* that same month, Burroughs finally quit peddling pencil sharpeners entirely and became a full-time writer. In the copybook way he sometimes talks, Burroughs modestly shares the credit for having found himself, "I am convinced that what is commonly known as the breaks, good or bad, have fully as much to do with one's success or failure as ability," meaning, perhaps, that all the bad breaks added up to a good one.

Once he got going, Burroughs had no trouble keeping up production. Ideas came from everywhere. One day in 1921, for example, he read a piece on the Life of the Mole and his imagination took it up from there. Why couldn't two red-blooded fellows named David Innes and Abner Perry get lost driving a subterranean vehicle named The Iron Mole in search of new coal veins, and find adventure and love in that savage, primeval world that lies at the center of the earth, Pellucidar? Then, with no thought of narrative hooks, planting, suspense, or climax, he scribbled off the 80,000 words that made a book in a month's time. Through with it, he re-scanned only to check for incongruities and misspellings. Rewriting he considered pretentious.

A short time ago, a young, aspiring writer asked him how he mastered his marvelous technique. "What technique?" asked Burroughs. When the y.a.w. looked nonplussed, Burroughs conceded, "I guess I was just a natural born storyteller. In medieval times I would have been a minstrel, except I can't carry a tune."

"But," the y.a.w. persisted, "in your last Tarzan book, for instance, no one knows Colonel Clayton is Tarzan for 78 pages. That's technique."

"Didn't you guess?" asked Burroughs delightedly. "Well, *that* is a trick. Let the reader think he's smarter than you—at least, than some of the characters, and let him guess something before it's revealed."

"How did you describe your places without doing any research?" asked the y.a.w.

"No research? What do you think I used those for?" said Burroughs, pointing to the shelves of books around him comprising one of the best private libraries of Africana.

The first Tarzan was written with only a 50c Sears dictionary and Stanley's *In Darkest Africa*, but, as he prospered, Burroughs accumulated material on his favorite place. Twenty-three Tarzan books and almost 40 years after becoming press agent for jungle life, however, Burroughs has never been to the dark continent, and he never hopes to go there. "I've seen more of Africa through the eyes of trained observers than I could have by going myself," he says. What he has done is the strongest argument yet advanced for the write-about-what-you've-never-seen school. Whenever Robert Thompson, an ex-pulp writer who does the continuity for the newspaper Tarzan strip, gets stuck, he consults a Burroughs book. Thompson once spent six months driving a truck from Capetown to Cairo, but he maintains the best African descriptions come out of Burroughs.

Henry Stanley's *In Darkest Africa*.

"And how did you ever think of so many new situations?" It was the y.a.w. again. "With so many books on the same subject," Burroughs 'fessed up, "I *had* to repeat myself, but generally I used different names and, while the critics might have minded, the loyal readers never did." In the 1947 Tarzan, for example, the jungle boy: (1) Fights to the death (a) a python, (b) a tiger. (2) Fights a huge ugly-tempered ape for the supremacy of the tribe. (3) Fights the same ape again because he was too lenient and didn't kill him the first time. (4) Rescues a white girl who has been captured by the ugly ape, saving her from the fate worse than death. (5) Rescues the white girl from another fate worse than death at the hands of savage Japs, etc., etc. Except for some tropical trappings, one might think he is reading the very first Tarzan all over again. Edgar Rice Burroughs has every right to be fond of his loyal readers.

It might be Tarzan; it might be David Innes; it might be Carson Napier rescuing Duare, "the sacrosanct daughter of an emperor, whom mortal man might not look upon and live" from the human amoebae of the city of Voo-ad on the planet Venus with the help of an amoebae who has fallen in love with Duare; it might be Gahan of Gathol rescuing Tara, of Helium, imperial daughter of the Warlord of Barsoom, from the headless Rykors and the bodyless Kaldanes of the land of

Bantoom on the planet Mars with the help of a Kaldane named Ghek who has fallen in love with Tara; it might be the Deputy Sheriff of Comanche County; it might be during the Stone Age or during World War II. But basically Burroughs wrote one book 57 times.

In one of the books two fellows who took familiar to each other meet in a jail in Manator.

"And who are you?" asked Turan.

"I am A-Kor the Dwar, keeper of the Towers of Jetan," replied the other. "I am here because I dared speak the truth of O-tar the Jeddak. And you?"

"I am Turan the Panthan who was chained beside you."

A-Kor looked at him closely. "Your own mother would never know you!" he said.

It is just that incongruity of the grotesque and the commonplace that are fused in Burroughs. He is a man of paradoxes—a born writer with no literary pretensions, loving solitude, and a true family man. Working at home, he always had a lot more time to give his children than the father who punches a time-clock.

When the children were very small, it was Burroughs' job to tell them bedtime stories and, after a hard day's writing, pacing in the corridor outside their rooms, he broadcast improvisations wholesale. Characteristically, he had several serials going at the same time. In one of them, "Grampa Kazink and his Flying Machine," Grampa, something of an interplanetary superman on a child's level, was constantly rescuing his girl friend, Ara Bella, from other-world savages. After Burroughs had worked the kids up to an unbearable pitch, with Grampa hanging on to the edge of Mars while six-legged Moaks hacked away at his tiring fingers, he would call, "That's all, children. Now go to sleep." It still gives them insomnia when they think of it today.

Even when Burroughs worked at the commercial adult product, the children played under his feet, interrupting to ask such questions as: "Why is the sky blue?" Son Hulbert was well on in years, he says, before he ever thought of consulting the Book of Knowledge.

The Burroughs family always did things as a unit. In 1916, the year of *The Beasts of Tarzan*, they drove pioneer-style across the continent. Mr. Burroughs, who was suffering from neuritis, his wife and three children, then 8, 7, and 3, headed the caravan in a Packard, while a chauffeur, maid, Airedale, and canary followed in a truck that had been fixed up to look like a covered wagon. The chauffeur spent more time on side trips for auto parts than he did proceeding ahead, and one morning they woke to find he had taken French leave. Burroughs, neuritis, and all, had the whole caboodle on his hands. It took them a full three months to get to California. In 1919, the year of *Jungle Tales of Tarzan* and *The Warlords of Mars*, Burroughs bought a 550-acre ranch, a long safari into darkest San Fernando Valley in those days, named the place Tarzana and transferred operations.

The creator of Tarzan was for the first time in a natural habitat. On the desert soil, he tried raising Berkshire hogs, goats, cows, and potatoes, but lack of agricultural success didn't phase him. The whole family operated like a cavalry unit,

PULPFEST 2012

AUGUST 9-12

at the HYATT REGENCY~COLUMBUS, OHIO

— Celebrating —
100 YEARS OF
EDGAR RICE BURROUGHS'
JOHN CARTER
WITH OUR GUEST OF HONOR
MIKE RESNICK
HUGO & NEBULA WINNER!

— Featuring —
DAVID SAUNDERS
ON THE ART OF
J. ALLEN ST. JOHN

— Plus —
CONAN'S 80TH
COMMEMORATED WITH
JIM & RUTH KEEGAN
AND **MARK SCHULTZ**

— Amazing —
DEALER ROOM!
WITH PULP MAGAZINES
HARDCOVERS & PAPERBACKS
VINTAGE COMICS & ARTWORK
MOVIES, OTR AND MUCH MORE

— Visit **PULPFEST.COM** FOR MORE INFORMATION
OR EMAIL JACK@PULPFEST.COM FOR REGISTRATION AND UPDATES
OR WRITE: JACK CULLERS, 1272 CHEATHAM WAY, BELLBROOK, OH 45305

Artwork courtesy of The Korshak Collection & Vanguard Press, publishers of The Paintings of J. Allen St. John. John Carter TM Edgar Rice Burroughs, Inc.

climbing out of bed and onto horses by five in the morning. On a blackboard near the stables, the earlier starters left a notation of which trail they were taking. Burroughs became Tarzan on horseback, riding off before sunrise, an army .45 in his holster, shooting at rattlers and coyotes and often having the horse drop as if dead on him. After rolling free and watching the horse run off, Burroughs would walk back to the ranch. "Ah, that was living," he says.

After his second marriage in the mid '30s, when *Pirates of Venus, Tarzan and the Lion Men, Lost on Venus, Tarzan and the Leopard Men, Swords of Mars*, and *Tarzan's Quest* were appearing, Burroughs, now living in and Honorary Mayor of Costa de Malibu, became something of a social lion, and moved in a circle where, according to his Martian hero, Gathan of Gathol, people "can tell you exactly how the loin of the thoat should be prepared and what drink should be served with the rump of the zitidar." Burroughs had all the natural qualifications. He played anagrams, of course, with the case of Tarzan swinging through the trees, his bridge was of championship caliber, and the ham in him rose to the surface for charades.

However, social lion or no, a leopard man doesn't change his spots and whenever his more primitive self got the chance, it would roar its way to the fore. California suffered its last bad earthquake in '36. People huddled in their houses holding onto tables while Californian ceramics crashed about them. Suddenly a staunch figure in whipcord pants and leather puttees appeared—like Tarzan and/ or John Carter, Carson Napier, and David Innes—dashed in, and turned off the gas. It was Edgar Rice Burroughs, grinning widely. "Why, we could all be blown up," he said happily.

During the floods of '38—there's always something doing in California— valley people were desperately bailing out when the figure in whipcord pants and leather puttees appeared. This time Burroughs was carrying a picnic basket. "Hungry?" he asked, as he settled in the wet and spread out a very adequate lunch. Then he focused his camera and shot a roll of pictures.

After Tarzan reveals—in *Tarzan and the Foreign Legion*, the last of the Burroughs books there is going to be—that he is the possessor of eternal youth, he goes on to depreciate its possession. "Death has many tricks up his sleeve besides old age." "Maybe," suggests another character, "you'll just fall to pieces all at once like the one hoss shay." It is very likely Mr. Burroughs feels this is what happened to him. "I aged more in my 70th year than I did in the 69 preceding," he occasionally tells people. "I was a damn fool. I ran up and down ships ladders, having a good time, a man my age, too dumb not to know better." In '45, while still a correspondent Burroughs suffered a heart attack and had to be transferred back to Pearl Harbor and his days of high adventure were over.

Although, at first glance, Burroughs still looks at least a spry 15 years younger than he is, a closer examination reveals the drag of his gait and the palsy-like trembling of his hands as he lights one cigarette after another. "I yawn when I wake up and I keep yawning all day long," he says of his typical day. "I have a nice comfortable easy chair in my house I sit in. After I get tired of that, I get in my car and drive to my office where I have a nice comfortable easy chair I sit in. Every day I think I might start writing again but thinking about it alone wears me out."

This doesn't mean that from now on Tarzan's activities will be frozen into the time-machine. Realizing in 1923—the year *Tarzan and the Golden Lion, Pellucidar*, and *The Girl from Hollywood* were published—that his creation was going to be an exceptionally hardy perennial, Burroughs formed Edgar Rice Burroughs, Incorporated, and began publishing and distributing the books himself as fast as he could write them, as well as seeing personally that Tarzan's name was not taken in vain and without a contract by any novelty maker.

The business of manufacturing new Tarzan stories—outside of the books, not one grunt of which was ever ghosted—goes on. The latest movie script, *Tarzan's Magic Fountain*, was done by Curt Siodmak who wrote *Donovan's Brain*, a modern horror classic, and invented the wolfman for lucky Universal Pictures. Siodmak didn't consult with Burroughs and the new business he has devised for Tarzan and Cheeta, Tarzan's pet chimpanzee (who, incidentally, receives twice the salary the new Tarzan, Lex Barker, does) will be as much a surprise to Burroughs as to any kid in the audience.

On the other hand, what Tarzan went through on the comic pages, rescuing a white girl from the savage Men of Kohr, didn't surprise Burroughs at all. Once a week, Robert Thompson takes a batch of four Sundays and four dailies over to the Tarzana office for checking. After ERB, Inc. is satisfied that Tarzan is neither maimed or ridiculed, the continuity goes to the United Features Syndicate in New York and on to artist Burne Hogarth who turns Thompson's words into the rippling anatomical wonders you see on the comic pages.

Even without all this fresh activity, Tarzan would persevere. Just last year ERB, Inc. reissued 22 of the Tarzan, Mars, Venus, and Earth's Core (the 1930 amalgamation found *Tarzan at the Earth's Core*) series in new dollar editions. As Burroughs himself says uncomprehendingly, "The books are selling better than ever." ERB, Inc. goes along with very little supervision from Burroughs. C.R. Rothmund, business manager for 22 years, makes royalty and translation deals, fills book orders, and keeps tabs on every cent owing and due, assisted by Mildred Bernard, who for 12 years took Burroughs' books down in shorthand—or off the dictaphone—and typed them up for the printers in Kingsport, Tenn.

When *Tarzan of the Apes* was first published as a book in 1914, the *Nation's* reviewer said: "Only persons who like a story in which a maximum of preposterous incident is served up with a minimum of compunction can enjoy these casual pages." Since then, critics, when they bothered at all, harped on Burroughs' lack of background, taste, and grammar, adjudging his work banal at best. Burroughs has humbly agreed, at the same time trying to explain the fact that the work has grossed more than 100 million dollars for everyone involved and around 10 million for him.

"I'm just an average person," he says on numerous occasions, "and I guess anything that interests me should interest others. My books sell and entertain. That's all they're intended to do. Perhaps other people were caught in the same unbearable daily situation I was. It turned out they wanted the same kind of escape and were willing to pay a couple of dollars twice a year for it. That's the whole appeal in a word: escape."

In the matter of identification, the necessary vehicle for escape, Burroughs believes Tarzan wins readers and audiences by being what they'd like to be. Tarzan is strong, never sick, and unimpeachably square-shooting.

Curt Siodmak, a good movie writer, has thought up a switch. Besides everything else, Tarzan's one other thing most people would like to be: antisocial. "Tarzan and Rankin come from the same home town," he points out. Tarzan just wants to be alone in his own bailiwick. Other people wander in and he helps them with their problems mainly to get rid of them. What's more, he has a beautiful girl around—Jane, his wife.

On the screen, Cheeta, Tarzan's chimpanzee, is for the kids and the beautiful girl for their fathers, making what the reviewers call a family picture. Burroughs agrees on the value of this single blessedness. "The one mistake I made with Tarzan," he

Curt Siodmak, novelist and sreenwriter.

says, "was to have him marry in his second book." He was wise enough, however, not to dwell on this alliance in later books. A general moral tone may be all right, but replacing one of the shackles that had been removed from the reader in helping him to escape from himself wasn't.

Burroughs now lives in a modest ranch-style home on Zelzah Avenue—a name he didn't coin—in Encino, a residential suburb for the movie colony, a mile from his office in Tarzana—the town of 6000 that grew out of his ranch of the '20s. His housekeeper, Margaret, babies him as if he were a bright spoiled boy. "She's always complaining I don't eat enough," beams the 200-pound Burroughs. He spends a good part of his time in his den, not the sort of a lair you'd picture a primitive Tarzan living in, with its television set, bar, and nickel slot machine. So considerate a host is Mr. Burroughs that near the one-armed bandit is a box of nickels for the convenience of his guests. Burroughs, playing the machine, good humoredly gripes that it doesn't pay off enough and that his younger grandchildren insist on jamming it up with pennies.

Not long ago a couple of the few surviving old friends of Burroughs looked him up. The sight of them depressed him for days afterwards. Daughter Joan, the closest person in the world to him, thinks that he is just incapable of assuming the old man's way of looking at things. "Old people are too stodgy and conservative," she says. "They haven't had a new idea in 20 years. Maybe that's why Papa prefers people at least 20 years younger than himself. He doesn't get around much any more, but his mind is as quick as ever."

Burroughs, always an Anglophile—don't forget, Tarzan was really Lord Greystoke—has for an unimagined hero, Winston Churchill. "There's a great

man," he says "and he's a year older than I!"

Part of Burrough's days go into reading old favorites—non-fictional works on Africa and other relatively uncivilized places, and a new favorite, the fact detective magazines.

With a single exception, Burroughs never reads any fiction, which he still considers "silly." Of late, he's even begun to lose some of his respect for fact detectives. "Take this story," he complained to a guest. "It says the Chief of Police tilted back in his chair, put his feet on the desk, bit off the end of a cigar, and looked up at the ceiling . . . How in the heck would the writer know *that*? It's just silly."

Getting fed-up about a year ago, Burroughs wrote a crime story of his own, cramming into its short length 27 corpses including the detective. The story was written just because Burroughs didn't happen to be writing anything else at the time and was for private circulation only. Even when he isn't writing anything else, Burroughs is writing his diary, which is also somewhat influenced by his reading. "Nothing at all happens to me," he says, "but if I'm ever arrested for murder, I can prove I wasn't there."

The one exception to his ban on fiction is his own work. Until now he never reread the stuff after writing it, and it all seems new. There are certain passages that amaze him. "Could I ever have written that?" he says he asks himself. "It's really quite good. Not as silly as a lot of other fiction."

Burroughs was in his den the other day, musing with a much younger guest over the changes he's seen in three-quarters of a century. Suddenly the talk, as it often does now, turned to old age and its unexpectedness. Clenching his big fists, Burroughs grimly said, "I hate old age! Damn old age! I hate dull, old people and I hate death!" In the calm that followed this outburst, Mr. Burroughs tried to make his visitor feel more a part of things. "Still you might go before me," he pointed out.

· · · · ·

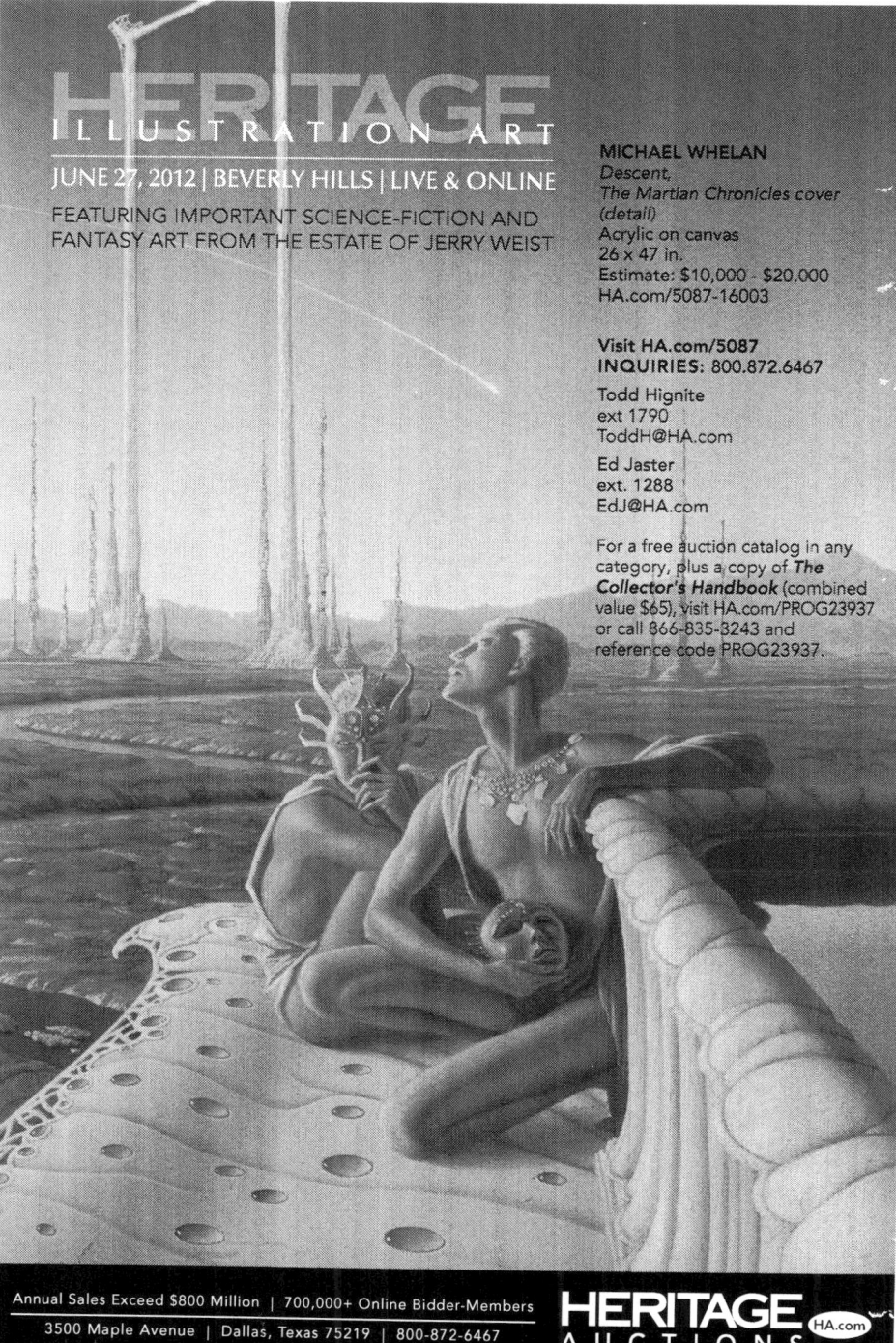

Meet the Authors

We present here an autobiographical sketch of Edgar Rice Burroughs, popular author of the John Carter stories now running in our pages

IN the first place, I don't like this assignment. If I tell the truth about myself, it will make dull reading. If I tell all the truth, it will be very embarrassing for me. But who ever takes his hair down and tells all the truth about himself?

According to the orthodox and approved introduction to an autobiography, I should tell all about my birth; but unfortunately, or perhaps fortunately, I can recall absolutely nothing about it: I don't even know that I was there.

Another cruel thing about an autobiography is that one is supposed to tell the exact date of one's birth. Oh, well, what's the difference? I was born on Wednesday. I think I got around that very neatly, for how many of you know that September 1st, 1875, fell on a Wednesday?

But I can go back much farther than that: my first ancestor of record (barring Adam) was Coel Codevog, King of the Britons, who ruled in the third century. There! You see it was just as I suspected: as soon as you start writing your autobiography, you start bragging. You don't say a word about Stephen Burroughs who was such a notorious forger and jailbreaker in early New England days that a book was written about him. I probably inherited my bent for writing from him.

Early childhood: Probably the less said about that the better. Fortunately for me, nearly every one who knew me then has carried his damning evidence to the grave. Let it lie and moulder: that will save me from lying.

Education: I had a lot of it, none of which stuck. After an advanced course in a private kindergarten, where I majored in weaving mats from strips of colored paper, I went as far as the sixth grade in the old Brown School in Chicago. That school has a roster that sounds like a Who's Who: Lillian Russell, Flo Ziegfeld, and dozens of others whose names I cannot recall. Then along came a diphtheria epidemic, and our parents yanked half a dozen of us boys out of public school and put us in Miss Coolie's Maplehurst

Mr. Burroughs at his desk in Tarzana, California

reprinted from *Amazing Stories,* June 1941

School for Girls! Were our faces red!

Miss Coolie endured us for one semester, after which most of us were sent to the Harvard School on the South Side. Somewhere along the cow path of my education I had a private tutor: then I was sent to Phillips Academy at Andover, Massachusetts. They stood for me for one semester before they asked my father to take me out of there.

He did. He took me to The Michigan Military Academy at Orchard Lake, Michigan, which had a sub rosa reputation as a polite reform school. I remained there four years as a cadet, ending up as second ranking cadet officer; then I went back as assistant commandant and cavalry instructor.

Somewhere along the line I went to Idaho and punched cows. I greatly enjoyed that experience, as there were no bathtubs in Idaho at that time. I recall having gone as long as three weeks when on a round-up without taking off more than my boots and Stetson. I wore Mexican spurs inlaid with silver: they had enormous rowels and were equipped with dumb bells. When I walked across a floor, the rowels dragged behind and the dumb bells clattered: you could have heard me coming for a city block. Boy! was I proud!

After leaving Orchard Lake, I enlisted in the 7th U. S. Cavalry and was sent to Fort Grant, Arizona, where I chased Apaches, but never caught up with them. After that, some more cow punching; a storekeeper in Pocatello, Idaho; a policeman in Salt Lake City; gold mining in Idaho and Oregon; various clerical jobs in Chicago; department manager for Sears, Roebuck & Co.; and, finally, Tarzan of the Apes.

For thirty years I have been writing deathless classics, and I suppose that I shall keep on writing them until I am gathered to the bosom of Abraham. In all those years I have not learned one single rule for writing fiction, or anything

EDGAR RICE BURROUGHS

else. I still write as I did thirty years ago: stories which I feel would entertain me and give me mental relaxation, knowing that there are millions of people just like me who will like the same things that I like.

The readers of this magazine have been very generous to me, and in return I try to give them the best that I can. No man can ring the bell every time; but he can always try; and your generous support, as evidenced by the letters you write to the editor, are, I can assure you, an incentive to a writer to do his best for you.

(Editor's Addenda: During the past few months, with the publishing of "John Carter and the Giant of Mars" in our January issue, we began a new series of Burroughs novels, to continue until early in 1942. During this time we will publish in all, five stories of the immortal John Carter (which, says Mr. Burroughs, will later appear in book form as the finest of the series of Mars stories); and four stories in the Pellucidar series, featuring David Innes in that strange world inside the earth. Simultaneously, in our companion magazine, *Fantastic Adventures*, we will feature a series of four novels of the adventures of the popular Venusian character, Carson of Venus. Thus, with 1941, we will be presenting, with the exception of the famous Tarzan, all of the pseudo-science, fantastic characters of the world's greatest imaginative writer.

No other author has ever achieved the widespread circulation, over the entire globe, in so many different languages, that Edgar Rice Burroughs has reached. Literally millions upon millions of his books are on millions of bookshelves and in millions of memories. Here is a pulp writer who will live as long in the mind of old and young alike as pulp fiction will live.

AMAZING STORIES has published the work of this writer before. Notable examples are "Land That Time Forgot," published in February, March, and April, 1927, in serial form; and "The Master Mind of Mars," published in *Amazing Stories Annual*, in July, 1927, in complete form.

Thus, for fourteen years, we have been associated, and to judge from the praise that is being heaped upon his recent work, we will be associated for many more years.

It is interesting to note that most of these present stories were written, not at Tarzana, the famed ranch and post office that Tarzan built, but in the south seas, in Hawaii. Here where soft breezes sweep in from the sea, and warm sun beats down on green palms and yellow sand, have been born the most thrilling adventure stories of other worlds Mr. Burroughs has yet written. Long may you live, John Carter, Carson Napier, David Innes—and Edgar Rice Burroughs!)

Letters to ERB

Ed Burroughs, a former merchandising department assistant manager for Sears, Robuck Company, and agent for a pencil sharpener company, grew so disillusioned with his current state of life in the struggle to provide for his family that in July 1911, he felt compelled to put to paper a story idea that had been bouncing around in his head, if for nothing else than a bit of escapism on his own part from boredom. The plot told the fantastic story of a princess on a far away planet. As

Portrait of Edgar Rice Burroughs from 1912.

the manuscript pages began to stack up Burroughs, with the ever-present thought of financial need on his mind, wondered about the likelihood of selling such a story for publication.

One of the few markets of the day printing stories of the incredible was *The All-Story Magazine,* part of a line of six fiction titles published by the Frank A. Munsey Company. The novice Burroughs mailed a portion of his long manuscript "Dejah Thoris, Martian Princess" to New York on August 14, 1911, for their input, and patiently awaited a reply.

Porges records in *Edgar Rice Burroughs: The Man Who Created Tarzan* that the author later admitted his blatant ignorance and inexperience, sharing: "I had never met an editor, or an author or a publisher. I had no idea how to submit a story or what I could expect to get in payment. Had I known anything about it at all I would not have thought of submitting half a novel. I do not know that any writer has ever done it successfully before or since."

Burroughs soon discovered what he could expect when within a fortnight a letter arrived from Thomas Newell Metcalf, editor of *All-Story*. This missive prompted a reply on Burroughs' part and a series of letters ensued.

This early correspondence from Metcalf shares fascinating details into the development of Burroughs' early novels, and displays Metcalf's often-blunt opinions and suggestions.

THE FRANK A. MUNSEY COMPANY

Munsey's Magazine
The Argosy
The All-Story Magazine
The Scrap Book
Railroad Man's Magazine
The Cavalier

175 FIFTH AVENUE

NEW YORK

August 24, 1911.

Mr. E.R. Burroughs
2?? W. Kinzie St.,
Chicago, Ill.

Dear Sir:-

It is with considerable interest that I have read "Dejah Thoris, Martian Princess." There are many things about the story which I like, but on the other hand, there are points about which I am not so keen. Undoubtedly the story shows a great deal of immagination and ingenuity; but I am unable to judge of course, the total effect, on account of its unfinished condition. I think it is rather slow in getting under way and it seems to me that you treat too casually and vaguely Carter's leaving the earth and arriving upon Mars. Then you often fall into long-windedness and tell many things which seem to me to be unessential to the story.

You speak of the taciturnity of the Martians, yet you have one of the ladies tell a story of a couple of thousand words and often the Tharks talk to a great extent. Somehow, it seems to me you are hardly consistent. As the story stands now it is not available, and any novel of 120,000 words would be twice too long. At the most we should not care to consider a story that was more than 70,000 words in length. If it would be possible for you to compress into that length a story as ingenious as is the greater part of what I have read, I should be very glad to consider it. I hope that you will think it worth your while, and I hope that you will give me a chance to look at the finished manuscript. I am holding the present m.s. at your disposal.

Very truly yours,

Thomas Newell Metcalf

THE FRANK A. MUNSEY COMPANY

Munsey's Magazine
The Argosy
The All-Story Magazine
The Scrap Book
Railroad Man's Magazine
The Cavalier

175 FIFTH AVENUE

NEW YORK

T.N.M.

New York, Nov. 4, 1911

Mr. E. R. Burroughs,
   222 W. Kinzie St.,
     Chicago, Ills.

Dear Mr Burroughs:

"The Martian Princess" story is in perfectly good form now and I should like very much to buy it for publication in The All-Story Magazine. I therefore offer you for all serial rights, $400.00.

As we, of course, do not publish books, this will leave all the book rights in your hands. If you do see fit to let us have this story, I should like to stipulate that I might change the title and that I shall very likely do some cutting especially at the very beginning of the story, and also very likely entirely eliminate Solar's story, as the latter does not seem to me to be necessary to the rest of the story.

I am sorry to have been so long in giving you an answer on this and I hope we will be able to do business together. While speaking of this, considering the fact that we have never done business together before, I should be very glad if you would send us a reference to some publisher or other responsible person who can assure us that your work is certain to be entirely original. This is a mere matter of form and I am sure you will understand how we feel.

I was thinking last night, considering with how much vividness you described the various fights, whether you might not be able to do a serial of the regular romantic type, something like, say "Ivanhoe", or at least of the period when everybody wore armor and dashed about rescuing fair ladies. If you have in mind any serials, or anything of that sort, and if you think it worth your while, I should be very glad indeed to hear from you in regard to them.

Very truly yours,

Thomas Newell Metcalf

Managing Editor,
THE ALL-STORY MAGAZINE.

M.H.

Metcalf's suggestion for "something like, say "Ivanhoe," prompted Burroughs to try his hand at historical fiction. In turn he wrote "The Outlaw of Torn," for *All-Story* which Metcalf then rejected.

THE FRANK A. MUNSEY COMPANY

175 FIFTH AVENUE

NEW YORK

Munsey's Magazine
The Argosy
The All-Story Magazine
The Scrap Book
The Railroad Mans Magazine
The Cavalier

T.N.M.

New York, November 20, 1911

Mr. E. R. Burroughs,
    Champlin-Yardley Co.,
        222 W. Kinzie St.,
            Chicago, Ills.

Dear Mr. Burroughs:

          I am sorry indeed to have been so slow in answering your letter of the 6th. In the story-writing game, as in any other game, it is efficiency that counts, and naturally if we discovered that stories written by you have the "punch" we should be very apt indeed to increase your rates. This sort of thing goes on right along, and many an author to whom we have in the beginning paid less than we do you, is making a very fair living by writing fiction.

          Of course a good deal more money can be made by a successful book, but considering the fact that every long story is, or should be written with book publication in mind, all monies recieved for serials, I should think, ought to be considered as velvet. That is the way we always look at it here, and we have at times been the greatest little incubator for best sellers that ever came over.

          The first installment of the story - and we are going to call it "In the Moons of Mars", will be the February All-Story. It was a mistake on my part that the formal endorsement on the check sent you was as it was. You need not worry, however, about losing the book rights. At any time when you feel that you want them, if you will drop me a line, I shall certainly see that they are immediately returned to you, and in the future should you sell us any more stories, I should be certain that whatever form of receipt you may sign will state that we are getting only serial rights.

          Very truly yours,

Thomas Newell Metcalf

MH

"The Martian Princess," Burroughs' second choice of a title for his manuscript, proves intriguing. Its initial magazine title, "In the Moons of Mars," was chosen by Metcalf, before appearing serially as "Under the Moons of Mars," beginning in the February 1912 issue of *All-Story*.

Burroughs did get his preferred title on the book version when the story appeared as *A Princess of Mars* from A.C. McClurg in 1917.

As history has shown, Burroughs' prudence in steadfastly selling only serial rights to the magazine publishers has proven a correct decision many times.

THE FRANK A. MUNSEY COMPANY

175 FIFTH AVENUE

NEW YORK

Munsey's Magazine
The Argosy
The All-Story Magazine
Railroad Man's Magazine
The Cavalier (Issued Weekly)

New York, June 26, 1912

T.N.M.

Mr. E. R. Burroughs,
    2008 Park Ave.,
       Chicago, Ills.

Dear Mr. Burroughs:

      I suppose by this time you have got a small souvenir from us to remind you of our attitude toward "Tarzan of the Apes".

      There are one or two things that I want to ask and suggest. In the first place, about your pen name. I have had a number of letters saying that people were very keen for Mr. Bean and his story of Mars and asking if we will not run some more work of his. Of course, I realize that I made a big break when I changed that name from "Normal" to Norman. Do you think it would be advisable to run this story under the name "Norman Bean", or shall I ignore any requests for some of that gentleman's work and run it under "Normal Bean", or your own name? I am willing enough to abide by any decision you may care to make, but would like to take advantage of the popularity of "Under the Moons of Mars" so far as is possible.

      Let me please request you never again, under any circumstances whatsoever, to write on such appallingly thin paper as you did. By the time I had read the manuscript and various of our clerical department had performed whatever necessary stunts they have to do upon it, the manuscript looked like a very much disheveled cabbage. When I get through editing it and the linotype man gets hold of it, it is very doubtful whether it will be at all tangible.

      Also, in the future, let me suggest that you never write single space - always double, at least.

      With these very harsh admonitions I will close this letter I might add, however, that I expect to be in Chicago some time after the middle of August and I hope that if you are not away on your vacation at that time, I shall have the pleasure of meeting you and that we may have luncheon or some libation together.

                Very truly yours,

                Thomas Newell Metcalf

M.H.

Burroughs would soon reject any further use of the Normal (or Norman) Bean pseudonym, preferring his own name accompany all future work.

    Metcalf's admonitions of Burroughs' choice of material for and presentation of his manuscript for "Tarzan of the Apes" comes across as humorous in a strict teacher sense, but in all honesty Burroughs had little knowledge of the standard accepted practices of the writing game. Single spacing his manuscript was presumably a thought by the frugal Burroughs to save paper, nothing more.

THE FRANK A. MUNSEY COMPANY

175 FIFTH AVENUE

NEW YORK

T.N.M.

Mr. Edgar Rice Burroughs,
        2008 Park Avenue,
                Chicago, Ills.   New York, Oct. 11, 1912

Dear Burroughs:

          "The Gods of Mars" will go through all right and if events are
highly favorable you will possibly receive a check next Thursday. I think the
story is very entertaining. I noticed with considerable sinking of heart that
you do not name the chapters. You can do just as you think fit about fixing them
up. If you are lazier than I am you very likely will say "Oh, let Metcalf do it!"
Of course you will see I am entirely at your mercy.

          I shall be sending you today or sometime very shortly, most
probably under separate cover, or possibly in this envelope, a batch of letters
which I have received commending "Tarzan". You may have them for your own. Most
of them are going to be published in the All-Story for December. There are some
others which I shall very likely send you later. I am returning to you also those
letters which you were kind enough to send me.

          I have been thinking over the necessity of a sequel to "Tarzan"
and it certainly looks as though we ought to have one, don't you think so? Of
course, as you say, sequels are never quite as good as the originals, but with
such a howling mob demanding further adventures of your young hero, it looks to
me as though it would be a very good move to bring him again to the notice of the
great public.

          I have been wondering whether it would not be possible to have
him, after receiving his conge from the girl, make a stagger at being highly
civilized in some effete metropolis, like London, Paris or New York, where he
very quickly finds the alleged diversions of civilization to be only as ashes in
his mouth. Thereupon, he decides that the only thing he can do is to go back to
the woods and again rule the apes. Naturally, with the amount of civilization
which he has got hold of, he finds upon his return to the jungle that there is
small satisfaction in being king over a few animals. For a while, of course, he
tried to persuade himself into believing that he is happy once more. He very
likely develops extreme cruelty and runs the gamut of doing all kinds of almost
insane things with the various animals and also with the blacks.

          Then I was wondering whether it might not in some way be possible
to introduce a young woman, whose childhood and youth had been spent exactly as
had Tarzan's. She had been somehow marooned in the wilderness and, as Tarzan, had
grown up to be a savage. I suppose you will have to re-introduce for some reason or
other Clayton and his wife. I don't know exactly how.

          I don't offer this line of guff as anything more than a suggestion.
It may be that you may find in it something which your superior ability might whip
into shape. Think the matter over, anyway, and if you do get any definite story in
mind let me know and send me a simple scenario of your idea.

          It is very funny about Mr. Brown. I really am not sure of his where-
abouts, but he took your address with a great deal of care. However, he may not have
liked the stories of yours which I showed him and possibly he thought he would not
hurt your feelings by gratuitously looking you up and telling you he thought you
were more of a success as a cheesemonger than as a story writer. We, however, know
differently and have no doubts at all that the time will come when let alone naming
race-horses "Tarzan", the word "Tarzan" will become a generic term for anything that
is a huge success.

                              Very truly yours,

                         Thomas Newell Metcalf

N.H.

THE FRANK A. MUNSEY COMPANY

175 FIFTH AVENUE

NEW YORK

T.N.M.

Mr. E.R. Burroughs,
    2008 Park Ave.,   New York, Jan. 27, 1913
    Chicago, Ills.

My dear Burroughs:

   I have given "The Ape Man" very careful consideration and I am very much
afraid that as it stands I cannot use it. This makes me feel very bad, because
of corse I was very keen indeed, both for your sake, for mine and for the sake
of all those insistent readers who wanted a sequel to "Tarzan".

   I fear, however, that the first 138 pages of the story are really quite
unnecessary. The incident in Paris, while good enough by itself, really does
not advance the story to any extent, neither does the incident with dancing girl
and the Arabs. I do not see the exact necessity of your villian Rokoff, nor Lord
Tennington and Hazel Strong, or of more than one of the various sailing parties
of which you write. By this I do not mean the trips on board the private yacht
or the various times that various of your characters are on the sea.

   After Tarzan goes to Africa again the story pickes up although it seems to
me that you have not really done yourself justice with Tarzan as king of that
tribe of negros. As a matter of fact, it strikes me that the attack and pursuit
of the marauding Arabs is rather tedious. There is not sufficient variety there.
Especially is that so considering that there has been a good deal of fighting
with the Arabs in the earlier part of the story.

   I liked well enough your City of Riches which comes along later, although
I felt that perhaps it was not as highly original as other work of yours and
possibly it had a similarity of tone at least to some of your Martian stuff.
But that part of it,however, I am perfectly willing to let stand.

   This whole story is not well balanced because you must realize as well as
I that you have no right to spend so many thousands of words getting Tarzan to
Africa and so few thousands of words keeping him there and getting him out of
the place. Also you spend a great many too many words in describing the various
ship wrecks and things of that sort and when you finally get the various groups
in Africa, you more or less ignore them and hustle them along rather brutally.
As a matter of fact, in several of the last chapters the point of view and scene
shift so continually that it is rather hard to keep the interest.

   I believe that you ought to start the story with a chapter that is somewhat
like your chapter 12. Then you have Tarzan, Clayton and Jane separate. I should
think it would be perfectly good to have Tarzan hit New York, say for a night.
In his lack of sophistication and in his grief, he might really get on a terrific
bender. Under the influence of liquor he might muss up the place or something of
that sort, but when the authorties looked after him they were only to willing
to deport him as an undesirable alien. All this makes civilization extremely
hateful to him.

   He might be met by D'Anot, at Havre, who argues with him regarding his re-
nunciation of Jane, and then supplies him with enough cash to find his way back
to Africa. D'Anot might apparently dislike the idea of Tarzan again reverting to
savagery and Tarzan might, to ease his mind, agree not to stay long in the jungle,
but go seemingly after the treasure which he might say he will bury in some place
not very far from the original cabin. A long time might go by and D'Arnot not
hearing from Tarzan and believing him very likely dead, might write to Jane or
might with Jane and Clayton charter a steamer, or something of that sort, and go
after the treasure themselves. In the meantime Tarzan has returned to savagery.
Of corse, when Clayton, D'Arnot and Jane arrive again at the jungle they may
have certain adventures. Tarzan by this time is thoroughly a savage.

   That is all I can think of just now. My particular point is, as I think I
said in a letter I wrote to you a while ago, that the interest in the former story
was in the jungle part of it and in the ingenuity that you displayed. Of course in
a story of this sort not so much ingenuity could be shown, but you had a perfectly

good motive before in describing Tarzan's gradual rise toward civilization. I
think you must have a motive in every story, certainly you have not one here as
it stands. It seems to me that as good a motive as any would be Tarzan's attempt
to become a savage again after deciding that civilization was no good, and his
final failure to become an animal again.

It may be that you will find these suggestions of mine thoroughly unsatis-
factory. I don't think they are particularly brilliant myself. At the same time,
I believe they are nearer what is necessary than the exploits through which you
run your hero in the present novel. There is too much shift of scene, too great
a cast of characters and no direct motive, and after you have played very hard
with certain people you submerge them and never think of them again.

Also 95,000 words are altogether too many for me. At the most, I really
cannot run more than 85,000. If you want to fix this thing up for me, and you
know I will only be too delighted if you will, I wish you would make a point of
not having it more than 80,000. I know you will appreciate how regretful I am
to have to return the manuscript and how hopeful I am that you will fix it up so
that I may not be dissappointed.

Very truly yours,

Thomas Newell Metcalf

Editor,

M.H.   THE ALL STORY MAGAZINE
P.S. The manuscript is being returned to you by express prepaid.

Burroughs had placed his faith and trust in Thomas Newell Metcalf's judgment,
believing his support, input and guidance added to the success of Burroughs' early
novels. So Metcalf's rejection of "The Ape Man" must have come as a shock

to the writer. While Metcalf had rejected
Burroughs' manuscript for "The Outlaw
of Torn," he had specifically requested a
sequel to "Tarzan of the Apes" from its
author. This rejection would prove a bless-
ing in disguise, prompting ERB to exam-
ine markets outside the Frank A. Munsey
Company, and opening a relationship with
All-Story's competitor, *New Story Magazine*, part of the Street & Smith line. Editor A.L. Sessions wrote to Burroughs on
February 8 accepting "The Ape Man" for
New Story, offering a higher word rate,
with Burroughs receiving $1,000 for the
serial rights.

Metcalf was eventually fired from
All-Story for letting the competition get
Burroughs' work.

"The Ape Man" appeared in hardcover under the title *The Return of Tarzan.*

Cover art by N.C. Wyeth.

A MARTIAN GLOSSARY

(The All-Story, October 1913, From the column "All-Story Table Talk")

. . . It looks very much as though Mr. Burroughs [will] hand us, one of these days before the snow flies, a third Martian story. Such being the case it has struck us as being worthwhile to compile a glossary of Martian terms.

Mr. Burroughs had all the terms at hand, and we simply put them in alphabetical order and are printing them hereinafter, so that all who read the Martian stories may know exactly what is what.

PROPER NAMES

Barsoom .... Mars.
Dor .... the Valley of Heaven.
First Born .... a black Martian race
Golden Cliffs...... the walls of the Otz Mountains, facing the Valley Dor.
Hastor .... a city of Helium
Helium................ the empire of the grandfather of Dejah Thoris.
Illall .... a city of Okar.
Iss .... the River of Death.
Issus................... the Goddess of Death.
Kadabra .... the capital of Okar.
Korad.................. a dead city of ancient Mars.
Korus.................. the lost sea of Dor.
Marentina .... a principality of Okar.
Okar................... the land of the Yellow Men.
Omean .... the buried sea.
Otz..................... the mountains surrounding the Valley Dor and Lost Sea of Korus.
Ptarth .... a Martian country.
Shador .... an island in the Sea of Omean.
Tenth Cycle .... a sphere or plane of eminence among the Holy Therns.
Thark .... a Martian city; also a Martian horde.
Holy Therns........ a Martian religious cult.
Thuria................ the nearer Martian moon.
Warhoon............. a community of green men inimical to Thark.

COMMON NOUNS

apt...................... a Martian arctic monster.
banth.................. a Martian lion.
calot................... a Martian dog.
dator .... chief or prince among the First Born.
darseen .... a Martian chameleon.
dwar................... a captain.

jed...................... a king.
jeddak.................. an emperor.
hekkador............. a father of therns.
kaor .... a form of greeting.
omad................... a man with only one name.
orluk .... a Martian arctic monster.
padwai .... a lieutenant.
pimalia................ a gorgeous flowering Martian plant.
sak .... a jump.
silian................... a slimy reptile inhabiting the lost Sea of Korus.
sith...................... a hornetlike monster.
skeel .... a Martian hardwood.
sorapus .... a Martian hardwood.
sorak................... a little pet animal among Martian red women about
                         the size of a cat.
tal........................ a Martian division of time corresponding to a
                         terrestrial second.
thoat.................... a green Martian horse.
thorian .... a chief among the lesser therns.
utan..................... a military company of one hundred men.
zad...................... a Tharkian warrior.
zat....................... a Martian division of time
                         corresponding to a terrestrial minute.
zitidar .... a Martian mastodonic draft-animal.
zode .... a Martian division of time
                         corresponding to a
                         terrestrial hour.

Roy Krenkel

Preparatory sketch for the cover of *Apache Devil*, Ballantine Books, 1975.
Pencil on tracing paper. Note the six gun on the floor left out of the final
painting due to time constraints.

TOM ROBERTS

An Interview With Artist Greg Hildebrandt

For nearly forty years, Greg Hildebrandt has been a leading name in the illustration and fantasy art fields. His paintings for the Lord of the Rings, Star Wars and Marvel Masterpieces, illustrated children's classic books, movie posters and paperback covers, and more recently, pin-up art, have inspired future generations of artists with his dazzling use of light and color.

Greg took a few moments to sit down and discuss his Burroughs cover art from decades past.

TR—*During 1975 Ballantine Books was releasing new editions of the Edgar Rice Burroughs novels. You and your brother Tim together received the assignments to provide cover art for two Burroughs titles, Apache Devil and The War Chief. These assignments, particularly being Westerns, were very different from the other cover jobs you were receiving from Ballantine. How did these assignments come about?*

GH—At that time, Ian Summers, was the art director at Ballantine Books. At one of the meetings Tim and I were having with Ian on the Lord of the Rings he mentioned the Burroughs books. We always loved Burroughs' books so we asked about the covers. Ian gave us two to do.

TR—*Although the two paperbacks were released in October 1975, the illustrations had obviously been completed months before. Were these painting done in between your Lord of the Rings and other fantasy illustrations?*

GH—Yes, we were working on the first Lord of the Rings calendar artwork when we did the Burroughs covers. As usual in the publishing industry they needed the art yesterday. So I posed my brother Tim for all the characters in both covers. I had to enhance his physical structure since Tim was a tall skinny guy and really didn't have the physique of an American Indian. We had a lot of fun painting those pieces.

TR—*Being a fan of Edgar Rice Burroughs novels, did you have any of the novels around your home as children?*

To see more of Greg's art, visit www.spiderwebart.com.

GH—Yes, my mother had all the Tarzan and Pellucidar books as well as John Carter.

TR—*Did you have a favorite artist that had illustrated the work?*

GH—J. Allen St. John. Is there anybody else?

TR—*Did Ian Summers provide you any type of art direction as to what he wanted on the covers? Any direction to go in?*

GH—No, Ian always left it up to the illustrator. That was one of the great things about him. He didn't over art direct.

TR—*These Burroughs covers were some of your earliest paperback cover assignments. Was there any look or style you were trying to capture with these pieces?*

GH—The first one *[Apache Devil]* was a style of Western pulp magazines of the 20s and 30s.

TR—*Drawn into your cover sketch for* Apache Devil *is a checkerboard-type grid. Would you explain what that was for?*

GH—We did not have the Xerox machine in those days and needed some manner to enlarge our sketch to the size we wanted to paint at. Using a grid accomplished this. It's a very old technique dating back to the Renaissance.

TR—*Have you done other Western illustrations? Is it a genre you are interested in or have pursued?*

GH—I have done very few pieces that deal with Western art. It is not an area that I have pursued because there are just so many days in a year. I do however love Western art.

TR—*With such a long career of being associated with and illustrating fantasy works, as well as many*

other type genres, if
the opportunity were to
present itself, would il-
lustrating the novels of
Edgar Rice Burroughs
now be an assignment of
interest to you today?

GH—I would certainly be interested in doing covers.
Illustrating full books
takes a lot of time and
my years are booked
very quickly.

TR—*Being aware that you
knew Frank Frazetta
personally, do you have
any reflections on his
Burroughs and related
illustrations?*

GH—Frazetta was a master at
what he did. His art will
live on for centuries.

TR—*What about other mod-
ern artists' interpreta-
tions of Burroughs sto-
ries such as Boris, Neal Adams, Michael Whelan, Joe Jusko? Any thoughts
on them?*

GH—Each of these artists bring something to their interpretation of the stories
that is unique and professional. My personal favorites are Hal Foster's Tarzan before Prince Valiant, Burne Hogarth's Tarzan after Hal Foster, Jesse
Marsh, Russ Manning and Joe Kubert.

TR—*Thank you, Greg, for taking the time to discuss your Burroughs work.*

GH—It's been my pleasure!

• • • • •

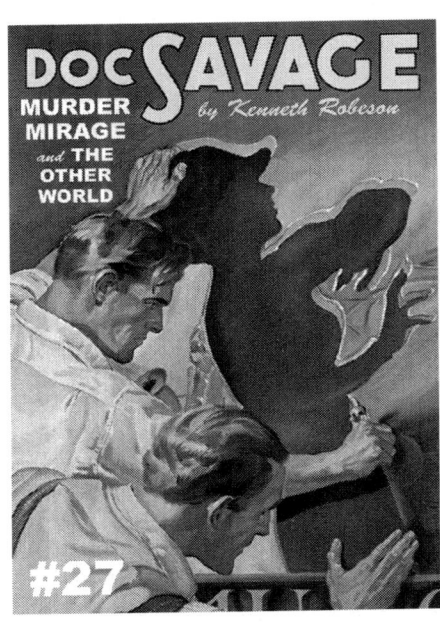
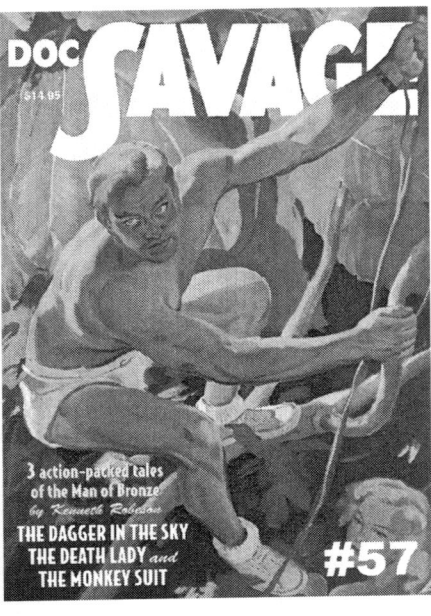
58

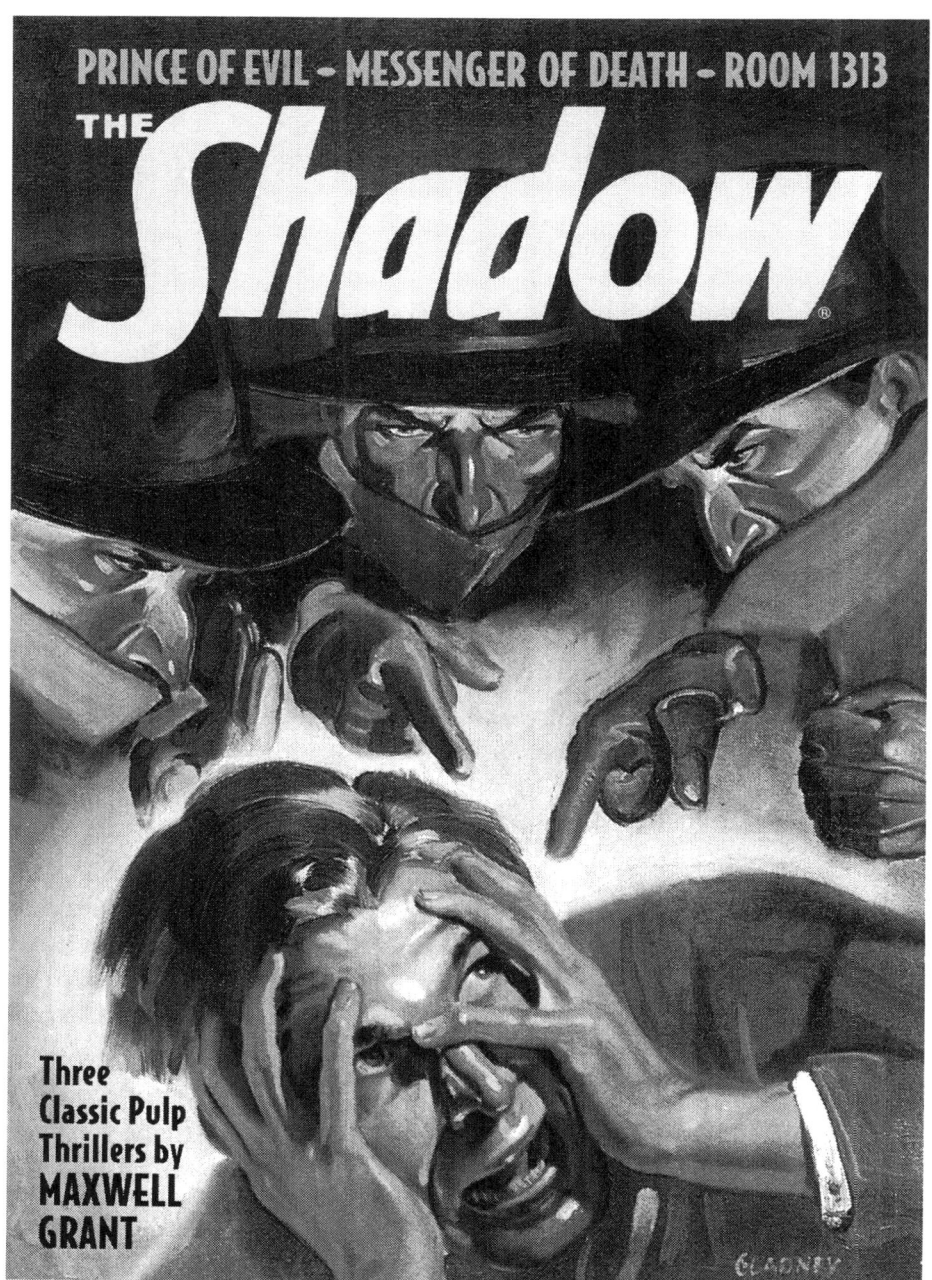

Watercolor preliminary study for "Chessmen of Mars." Previously unpublished.

DOUG ELLIS

A Brief Look at Roy G. Krenkel
and His ERB illustrations

"Roy Krenkel was a key factor in the 1960s revival of my grandfather's writings. Krenkel's illustrations forever secured his position as one of the all-time great Edgar Rice Burroughs illustrators."—Danton Burroughs

In any list of the great illustrators who have brought Edgar Rice Burroughs' fantastic worlds to life in paintings or pen and ink illustrations, Roy Krenkel must surely rank highly, in company with J. Allen St. John and Frank Frazetta. His work graces 24 published ERB books, 20 for Ace Books—beginning with *At the Earth's Core* in 1962—and four for Canaveral Press. All but two were published between the period 1962 to 1964. In addition to his ERB work, Krenkel also illustrated three books for Ace during the same period authored by one of ERB's contemporaries, Otis Adelbert Kline—*Planet of Peril, Prince of Peril* and *Port of Peril,* all of which were set on Venus. On the strength of his work for Ace, Krenkel won the Hugo Award in 1963 for Best Artist of the Year.

Krenkel came to the attention of Donald Wollheim, editor for Ace, through his illustrations for the Robert E. Howard related fanzine, *Amra.* For *Amra,* Krenkel contributed not only REH based material, but ERB based illustrations as well. His work for *Amra* and other fanzines ran the gamut from gorgeous, fully rendered pen and ink jewels to unpolished sketches, which still manage to convey a strong sense of movement and feeling. Krenkel's pen and ink work was masterful and most of the books he illustrated for Ace and Canaveral contain pen and ink interior illustrations.

In 1982, Krenkel's work was once more recognized, as the World Fantasy Convention presented him with a special award for his artistic contributions to the field.

Accompanying a list of Krenkel's professionally published ERB work for Ace and Canaveral Press are two preliminaries by him – for "The Chessmen of Mars" and "Out of Time's Abyss" – as well as a third preliminary piece, unidentified, showing two fighting men, one of who is mounted on a thoat, with the twin moons of Barsoom racing through the sky overhead.

ACE BOOKS PAPERBACKS (listed in publication order):

At the Earth's Core (1962, F-156)
The Moon Maid (1962, F-157)
Pellucidar (1962, F-158)
Thuvia Maid of Mars (1962, F-168)
The Chessmen of Mars (1962, F-170)
Tanar of Pellucidar (1962, F-171))
Pirates of Venus (1963, F-179)
The Mastermind of Mars (1963, F-181)
A Fighting Man of Mars (1963, F-190)
Tarzan Triumphant (1963, F-194)
The Land That Time Forgot (1963, F-213)
The People That Time Forgot (1963, F-220)
The Land of Hidden Men (1963, F-232)
Out of Time's Abyss (1963, F-233)
The Eternal Savage (1963, F-234)
Back to the Stone Age (1963, F-245)
The Cave Girl (1964, F-258)
Escape on Venus (1964, F-268)
The Outlaw of Torn (1968, A-25)
The Wizard of Venus (1970, 90190)

CANAVERAL PRESS HARDCOVERS:

The Cave Girl (1963)
Land of Terror (1963)
Tarzan and the Tarzan Twins (1963)
Tales of Three Planets (1964)

Acrylic preliminary study for "A Martian Scene." Previously unpublished.

Watercolor preliminary study for *Out of Time's Abyss,* Ace Books, F-233,
Previously unpublished.

Tarzan the Mighty

If Universal Pictures president Carl Laemmle had not been such an ardent prac-titioner of nepotism, his studio would never have produced the brace of Tarzan serials that enthralled moviegoers in the waning days of the silent-movie era and earned scads of money for Universal.

The narrative begins with Laemmle's brothers-in-law, Julius and Abe Stern, who followed the erstwhile clothing-store manager into the motion-picture busi-ness not long after he opened his first storefront theater in 1906. Reportedly, they were partners in Carl's Independent Moving Picture Company, which evolved into the Uni-versal Film Manufacturing Company. Some accounts credit them with helping Laemmle finance the 1912 purchase of the large North Hollywood tract—actually an old chicken ranch—that became Universal City. The Sterns

(Universal 1928)
Director: Jack Nelson
Stars: Frank Merrill,
Natalie Kingston

held various positions in the company during its formative years. In 1915, for example, Julius served as general manager of East Coast operations; at that time some Universal releases were still being shot in New York and New Jersey.

A year later, the brothers formed the Century Film Corporation, an indepen-dent production entity that supplied comedy short subjects for distribution by Universal. Then, in 1919, Julius and Abe partnered with Louis and Oscar Jacobs to create the Great Western Producing Company, which turned out several seri-als distributed by "Big U." These three chapter plays—*Elmo the Mighty* (1919), *Elmo the Fearless* and *The Flaming Disc* (both 1920)—starred Elmo Lincoln, the screen's original Tarzan.

Enter Louis, Max, and Adolph Weiss. Having crashed the movie business in 1917 as New York-based exhibitors, they formed the Numa Pictures Corporation two years later for the sole purpose of producing Tarzan films. From the ape-man's creator, Edgar Rice Burroughs, they licensed motion-picture rights to *The Return of Tarzan*, the second novel in the series. In an unusual deal, ERB gave Numa the option of making two films from the same book. The first—initially titled *The Return of Tarzan* but ultimately released as *The Revenge of Tarzan*—was distrib-uted by the Goldwyn Distributing Corporation, which paid Numa an advance of $100,000 for the privilege. The Weiss brothers were to receive a percentage of the film's profits as well, but Goldwyn's accounting of the revenues left something to

This article originally appeared in *Blood 'N' Thunder* no.24, and appears in revised form in Ed's book on silent movie serials, *Distressed Damsels and Masked Marauders*.

be desired and the siblings vowed to self-distribute their next Tarzan film.

Believing they could achieve better box-office results by returning Elmo Lincoln to the role that made him a star, the Weiss brothers engaged the Great Western Producing Company—which still had Lincoln under contract—to make their second *Return of Tarzan* adaptation. This time around they elected to produce a serial, which was titled *The Adventures of Tarzan*. They formed the New York-based Adventures of Tarzan Serial Sales Company to distribute the chapter play via the already-well-established "states rights" system, which allowed for the rental of prints to exhibitors by independent contractors (known as sub-distributors) on a territorial basis.

Released late in 1921, *Adventures of Tarzan* was extremely successful. The Sterns, still having Lincoln under their thumbs, decided they could do their own Tarzan films and bypass the Weiss brothers altogether, now that Numa had shot its bolt. In 1922, with *Adventures* still in theatrical playoff, Julius and Abe and Louis Jacobs paid Burroughs $40,000 for screen rights to *Tarzan and the Jewels of Opar* and *Jungle Tales of Tarzan*, the fifth and sixth books in the series.

Then fate stepped in. For reasons not clear today, the Great Western Producing Company dissolved shortly after this transaction. Elmo Lincoln suddenly found himself unemployed and reduced to taking supporting roles in such feature films as *Quincy Adams Sawyer* (1922) and *Rupert of Hentzau* (1923). He returned to the Universal lot, where he had been a star just a few years earlier, to play an unbilled bit part in Lon Chaney's version of *The Hunchback of Notre Dame* (also 1923). The newly acquired Tarzan option went unexercised.

Great Western's unexplained demise must have been a blow to the Sterns, but they still had steady income thanks to their brother-in-law: Carl Laemmle continued to distribute their Century Comedies, which were churned out by the dozen every year. Additionally, Julius returned to the ranks of Universal management and held several executive positions throughout the Twenties.

Movie serials diminished in stature and significance as the decade wore on, and although Universal maintained a healthy market share, its chapter plays rarely proved to be big grossers. (Two exceptions were 1924's *The Riddle Rider* and 1927's *Blake of Scotland Yard*.) But Laemmle, who prided himself on the diversity of Universal's extensive short-subject program, never lost faith in serials. Every season's offerings were announced to the trade with great fanfare and the promise that, in the year to come, chapter plays would be restored to the position of importance they had occupied in the halcyon days of *The Perils of Pauline*.

A story in the April 7, 1928 issue of *Universal Weekly* (the company's house organ, circulated to distributors and exhibitors) announced that the company had "just acquired rights" to ERB's *Jungle Tales of Tarzan*. A follow-up story in the April 28 number indicated that *Jungle Tales* would be filmed in 12 chapters and serve as the leadoff serial for the 1928-29 season. At this late date, it's not clear why the Stern brothers waited so long to relinquish their hold on *Jungle Tales*. Possibly they were inspired to dispose of the property in the wake of FBO's poorly reviewed but extensively promoted and generally successful 1927 feature

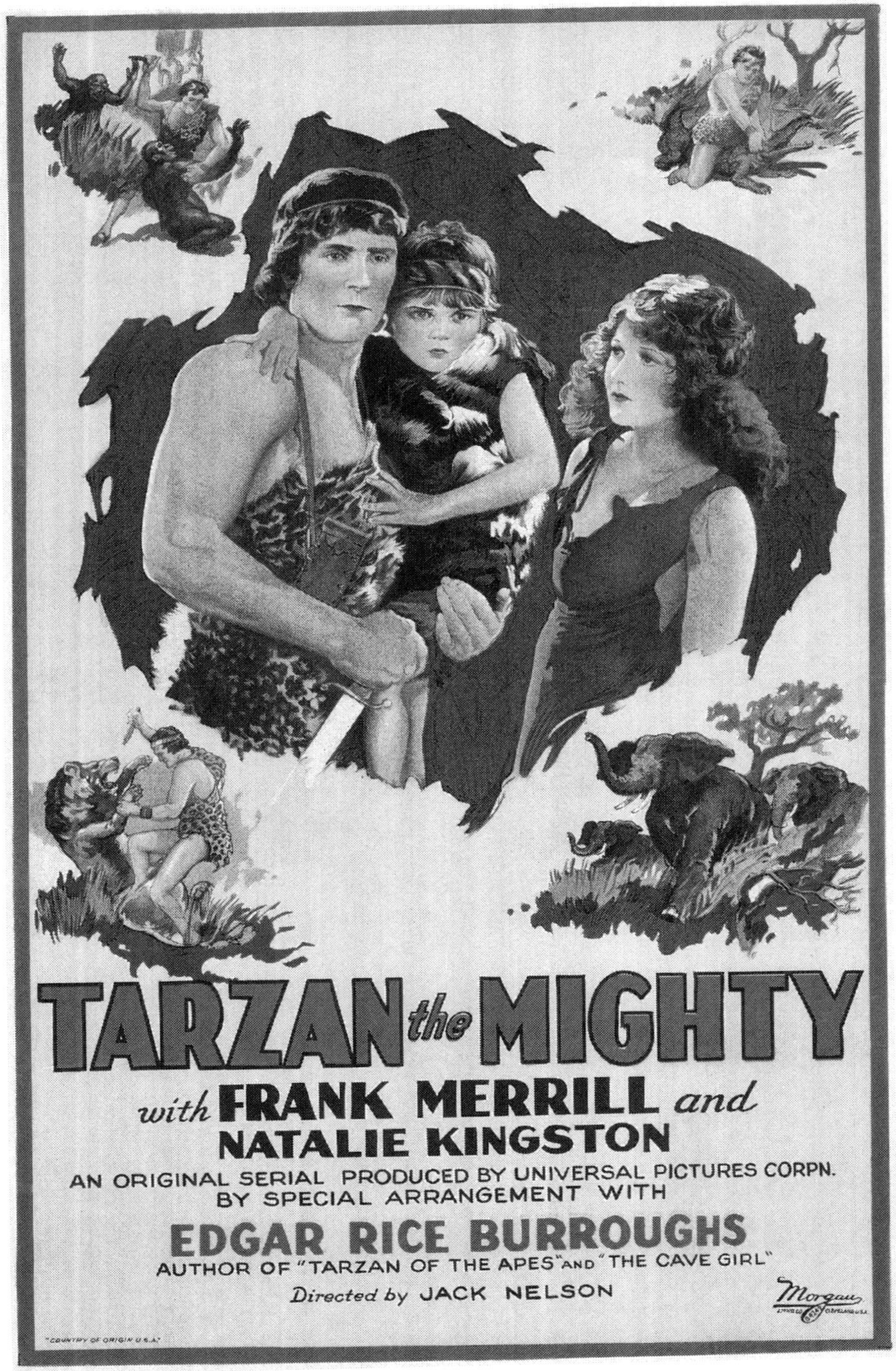
TARZAN the MIGHTY
with FRANK MERRILL and
NATALIE KINGSTON
AN ORIGINAL SERIAL PRODUCED BY UNIVERSAL PICTURES CORPN.
BY SPECIAL ARRANGEMENT WITH
EDGAR RICE BURROUGHS
AUTHOR OF "TARZAN OF THE APES" AND "THE CAVE GIRL"
Directed by JACK NELSON
Morgan

film, *Tarzan and the Golden Lion*. It could also be that the popularity of Grosset & Dunlap's inexpensively priced Tarzan reprints, then being issued on a regular basis, further enhanced the character's public profile and earning power. In any case, Laemmle paid his relatives for the motion-picture rights they held to ERB's works. Whether or not they made a profit or simply recouped their investment is anybody's guess.

Naturally, production would be overseen by William Lord Wright, the firm's serial czar. Direction was entrusted to Jack Nelson, who had recently helmed a 10-chapter serial, *Perils of the Jungle*, for none other than the Weiss brothers. Nelson was a newcomer to Universal City; a former actor, he cut his directorial eyeteeth on films made by the Thomas H. Ince organization but spent most of his career working for the independent production companies that comprised the lowest links on Hollywood's food chain. Nonetheless, he had done an excellent job on *Perils of the Jungle*, utilizing practically the entire menagerie housed at the Selig Zoo. Each chapter of *Perils* ended with cast members imperiled by wild beasts, and Nelson got the maximum number of thrills obtainable on what had to have been a modest budgetary outlay. He was obviously the right man for the job, but Wright was not about to grant directorial autonomy to a newcomer; Nelson would be joined on *Jungle Tales* by Ray Taylor, at that time Universal's serial ace.

The job of adapting Burroughs' book, a collection of short stories set during Tarzan's youth and early adulthood, fell to one Ian McClosky Heath, about whom nothing is known. Universal's two Tarzan serials are his only screen credits, and his name cannot be found on any roster of fiction writers plying their trade in the 1920s. Confronted with the impossible task of crafting a suitable serial plot from ERB's unrelated tales, Heath jettisoned the book and devised an original story.

In that same April 28 article designating *Jungle Tales of Tarzan* as the opening act in Universal's 1928-29 serial program, the anonymous scribe reported "a great rush on amongst the mighty men of Los Angeles to play Tarzan." There's no way of knowing exactly how many actors tested for the role, but the casting process could not have been a lengthy one: a squib in the May 19 *Universal Weekly* declared that Frank Merrill had just been signed as the ape man, and that filming would commence shortly.

One of the most persistent myths about Universal's first Tarzan serial is that the title role was originally awarded to Joe Bonomo, the New York-born strongman who had previously starred in two of the company's 1925 chapter plays, *The Great Circus Mystery* and *Perils of the Wild*. The innumerable, erroneous reports of Bonomo's casting all derive from passages that appeared in two books published almost simultaneously in 1968: Gabe Essoe's *Tarzan of the Movies* (New York: The Citadel Press) and Joe's self-published autobiography, *The Strongman* (New York: Bonomo Studios Incorporated).

Essoe's account had Bonomo bowing out after fracturing his left leg and injuring his sacroiliac shortly before completing work on *Perils of the Wild*. Inasmuch as *Perils* was shot fully three years before Universal's first Tarzan serial—a fact of which Essoe was apparently unaware—this report is easily discredited.

Bonomo's version of the story seemed somewhat more credible but hasn't held up to close scrutiny. He was vague as to the exact date but recalled being cast as Tarzan some six months before the expiration of his Universal contract. The way Bonomo remembered things, he was antsy to freelance but Laemmle wanted him to stay with the studio. In order to keep the stuntman-turned-actor busy pending the negotiation of a mutually acceptable deal, "Uncle Carl" (as he was by then known within the industry) assigned Joe the Tarzan role, released publicity pegged to his casting, and immediately began production on the serial. Bonomo claimed he fractured his left leg on the third day of shooting, falling heavily to the ground after a vine snapped while he was swinging from tree to tree. He added that production came to a halt and only resumed "much later on" with Merrill in the lead.

As proof, Bonomo reprinted in *The Strongman* one small news item, apparently clipped from a newspaper or trade journal. Seen today, it looks convincing enough. The headline proclaims: "Tarzan to Appear on Screen Again; Joe Bonomo Is He!" Undated and not bylined, the dispatch's first paragraph reads: "Those refreshing stories of jungle life by Edgar Rice Burroughs, which have thrilled children and adults alike, are again to appear pictorially, it was bruited yesterday, with none other than Joe Bonomo, who styles himself as 'the Hercules of the Screen,' in the role of the super-hero, for Universal."

There are several problems within Bonomo's account. To begin with, his last picture for Universal was an epic Western, *The Flaming Frontier*, released in September 1926. (It was, in fact, the only picture he did for the studio that year.) Assuming his contract had not yet run out, this would indicate that principal photography on *Jungle Tales* commenced nearly two years before it actually did. Secondly, close examination of Universal's yearly program announcements reveals no Tarzan serial on the 1925-26, 1926-27, or 1927-28 schedules. There's no way that any Hollywood studio would have rushed into production a chapter play featuring as well known a fictional character as Tarzan without considerable ballyhoo. Thirdly, even if Bonomo was wrong about the timing of *Jungle Tales*, he couldn't have spent three days shooting it in the spring of 1928, because at that time he was making *The Chinatown Mystery*, a Trem Carr-produced serial released by Syndicate Pictures only two weeks after Universal's first Tarzan opus hit theater screens.

The news clipping reprinted in *The Strongman* would seem to lend credence to Bonomo's version of the story, but it hardly supplies conclusive proof. No title is given. No dates are given. And the report maintains that Bonomo has been "bruited" as a possible movie Tarzan. As "bruited" is a synonym for "rumored," one could reasonably assume that, at the time of the article's appearance, Universal had contemplated but not actually scheduled production of a Tarzan serial. Remember, that April 7, 1928 news story reported that the company had "just acquired" rights to *Jungle Tales*.

Finally, there's this: I've yet to see mentioned anywhere in *Universal Weekly* a single mention of Bonomo being cast as Tarzan. Not in 1926, not in 1927, and certainly not in 1928. Had one of the company's former serial stars even been *considered* for the role, the house organ would surely have reported as much. Long ago I came to the conclusion that, while Joe might have discussed making a Tarzan serial for Laemmle, he was never actually cast—and that the injury he later recalled was actually sustained during production of *Perils of the Wild*, which also took place in a jungle and found Bonomo's character swinging from vines and leaping from tree to tree.

In short, there's a distinct lack of hard evidence to support the contention that anybody but Frank Merrill was awarded the title role in Universal's first Tarzan serial.

Born in 1893 as Otto Poll, the New Jersey native worked for several years as a police officer in the city of Newark before attempting to parlay his good looks and athletic ability into a movie career. A superb physical specimen who won dozens of gymnastics awards in competition, Poll was cited in a 1918 *New York Times* article as a "champion at flying rings." Not long afterward, he relocated to Los Angeles and became active in West Coast athletic circles. He secured bit roles and performed stunts in motion pictures (including *The Adventures of Tarzan*, in which he played an Arab heavy and doubled Elmo Lincoln in certain shots) but remained an active participant in gymnastic exhibitions. A 1922 *Times* article on upcoming events sponsored by the Amateur Athletic Union referred to him as a "famous gymnast from Los Angeles."

Poll took the name Frank Merrill upon being hired to star in the first of a dozen low-budget feature films for Hercules Film Corporation. Designed for un-discriminating audiences and employing simple, action-oriented plots, such pictures as *A Fighting Heart* (1924) and *Dashing Thru* (1926) gave the star athlete frequent opportunities to show off his impressive physique and gymnastic skills. He had more of the same as the hero of *Perils of the Jungle*, swinging through trees, dangling from gnarled limbs, and climbing vines hand over hand. It's no wonder director Jack Nelson wanted him for the role of Tarzan.

The next casting challenge, not surprisingly, was finding a suitable female lead to appear opposite Merrill. Heath's scenario stuck to ERB's book only to the extent that the action took place before Tarzan met Jane. The necessary heart interest was supplied by Mary Trevor, a young woman shipwrecked off the African coast and held prisoner by a tribe of savage white men descended from pirates. This was a key role; Mary would occupy the screen as much as the ape-man. An experienced actress would be required.

In mid-May, shortly after Merrill was signed, Natalie Kingston was cast as Mary. A lissome, leggy, olive-skinned brunette of Spanish and Hungarian descent, born in 1905, Kingston broke into show business as a dancer and enjoyed a brief, modest Broadway career before entering motion pictures in 1923. Never really a star, she played leads and supporting roles alike; shortly before accepting the role of Mary Trevor, Kingston finished a character part in Frank Borgaze's *Street Angel* and appeared opposite Western star Tom Mix in *Painted Post*. She had the necessary acting experience and looked fetching in abbreviated jungle garb.

Frank Merrill

Rounding out the small group of principal players were director Nelson's five-year-old son Bobby, who had appeared opposite Merrill in *Perils of the Jungle*, and Irish actor Al Ferguson, prolific heavy of late '20s Universal Westerns and serials.

With the cast finally in place, principal photography began immediately. *Jungle Tales of Tarzan* was dropped as a title in favor of *Tarzan the Mighty*, and Universal's publicity machine geared up to promote the serial. According to Irwin Porges' definitive biography, *Edgar Rice Burroughs, The Man Who Created Tarzan* (Provo, Utah: Brigham Young University Press, 1975), ERB visited the Universal lot to screen rough footage assemblies on June 14, 1928. Not entirely happy that long-dormant rights assigned to the Stern brothers were finally being exploited with no additional compensation to him, Burroughs chafed at the serial's deviation from the book on which it was ostensibly based. He enumerated his problems with the screened footage in a memorandum quoted by Porges:

. . . there was only one character that appears in the original work, namely Tarzan, and no suggestion of any episode or action taken from the book.

They have incorporated many characters, including a Lord Greystoke, some pirates, sailors, and castaway girl and her little brother, none of which appears in the original work.

They have incorporated a love interest between Tarzan and the girl, which does not exist in the book.

Burroughs had always been annoyed by Hollywood's treatment of his brainchild, and Universal's incarnation of the ape-man only exacerbated his disenchantment with filmmakers. He did, however, admit that the muscular, fierce-looking Merrill might make a good Tarzan. As a good-will gesture, the studio paid ERB $1,000 for newspaper syndication rights to *Jungle Tales*, even though the novelization being circulated was based on Heath's scenario and not the book. It was reportedly written by Craig Kennedy creator Arthur B. Reeve, who had recently scripted *Return of the Riddle Rider* for Universal. But it doesn't read like Reeve's prose, and I suspect the novelization was actually penned by a drone in the studio's publicity department.

(Universal used part of the novelization to good advantage as a promotional tool. A compilation of the first three chapters was made into an eight-page booklet of six by nine inches. Illustrated with stills from the film, this pamphlet was sold for six dollars per thousand copies to exhibitors who distributed it to potential customers. Circulated in advance of the serial's playdate, the eight-page prose "teaser" proved a tremendous drawing card. Since the booklets were giveaways meant to be discarded after reading, very few copies survived. Today they are expensive, highly sought-after collectibles.)

The June 30 *Universal Weekly* carried a news item stating that production of *Tarzan the Mighty* was nearly half-completed. The advance word was good; prominent exhibitors given previews of the first several chapters were uniformly enthusiastic, and even Uncle Carl had been impressed. He lauded the serial in one of his avuncular "Straight from the Shoulder" columns written for the house organ. Universal's sales department began taking orders from theater chains, including some that didn't normally run serials. Exhibitors who subscribed to the company's "Complete Service" plan (under which they paid a flat fee for a full annual complement of Universal feature films, short subjects, and serials) got *Tarzan the Mighty* at a bargain price, but those who normally shunned Laemmle product paid excessively for it. The heavily promoted chapter play was booked for big downtown houses in major metropolitan areas—movie palaces that seldom offered such lowbrow fare as serials. The prestigious Loew's chain, allied with no less a studio than Metro-Goldwyn-Mayer, scheduled it for their New York City flagship theater.

Exhibitors who weren't initially enthusiastic changed their minds once the early reviews broke in various trade journals. A mid-July screening of the first three episodes in Universal's New York office wowed even the most jaded critics. Industry veteran William Wilkerson, then editor of *Exhibitors Daily Review*, led the parade:

> We were greatly surprised. This [serial] is different and is going to have a wide appeal, in that it is going to create a new audience for this type of entertainment. . . . [Universal has] taken a story that is plausible, given it excellent direction and a superb cast. But the big kick of the chapters we saw were furnished by the animals. . . . Adults will go for this one with more interest (if possible) than the kids. They will not have to stretch their imagination to be entertained, nor will they snicker at the impossibility of the story or situations. The production values have lifted to the par of feature productions in that the sets and the camera work are superb. Exhibitors would do well to look at this one [at their local Universal exchange office] before booking it. They will forget about the 'for matinees only' and run it all day and maybe more.

Chester J. Smith of *Motion Picture News* was similarly effusive in his praise:

> This gives promise of being one of the most unusual serials yet produced. It is entirely out of the ordinary run of such pictures and should develop some highly interesting highlights before its conclusion. . . . There are some exceptional shots of the jungle and the wild animals, and they add greatly to the general effectiveness of the picture, which gives rare promise of developing into a tremendous thriller.

Over the years, chapter plays had drawn considerable criticism from watchdog groups believing them harmful to the children that comprised the lion's share of their audiences. *Tarzan the Mighty* got a clean bill of health from most of these, and was highly recommended by Mrs. E. H. Florence Jacobs of the California Federation of Women's Clubs:

> *Tarzan the Mighty* is an unusually fine serial, remarkably well told, full of action and exciting sequences, and is superior in direction, continuity, and photography to most serials. While we have only seen three chapters, I feel safe in saying this serial can be highly recommended for junior matinees, and we are looking forward to seeing the rest of it. It is a thrilling story, told in specially commendable titles in their presentation of suspense, which means so much in a serial of this type, and at the same time has no exaggerated criminal characters.

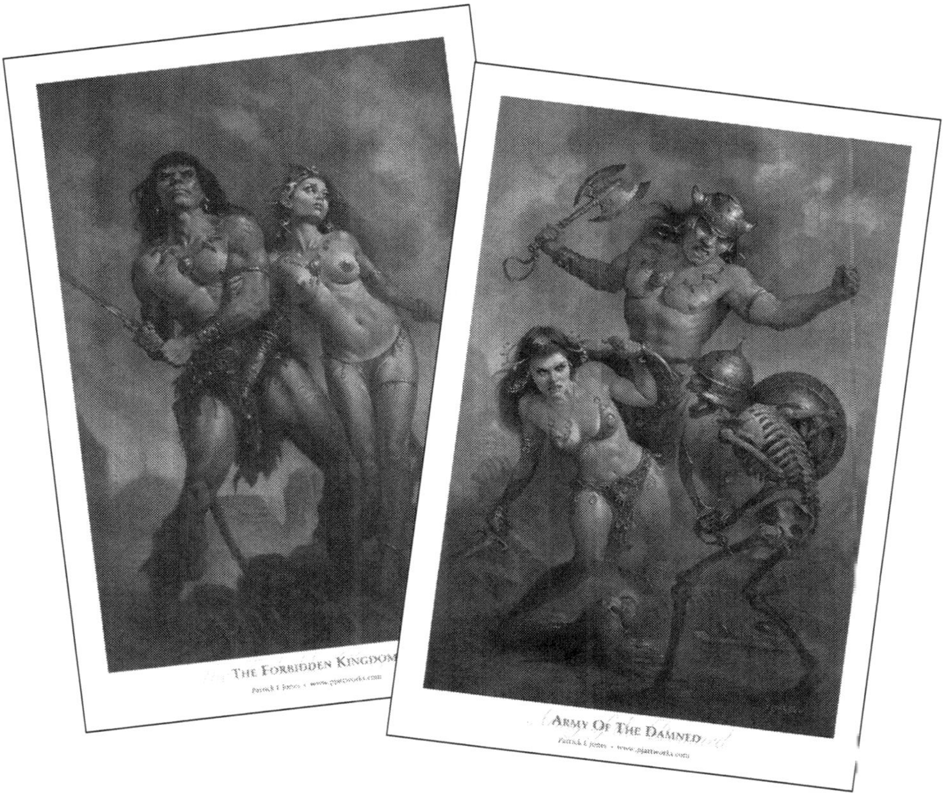

Tarzan the Mighty, like all but a few silent serials made by Universal, is a lost film. But one can reconstruct it, after a fashion, from careful readings of the Arthur B. Reeve novelization and the individual chapter synopses printed in Universal Weekly.

Chapter One presents the familiar Tarzan origin story: how his English parents, Lord and Lady Greystoke, were stranded on the African coast and forced to take shelter in a crudely built hut; how his mother and father perished, leaving him to be "adopted" by a she-ape; how he matured among the beasts of the jungle, forced by his savage upbringing to develop uncommon strength and agility; and how he learned rudimentary English by studying the books left behind in his parents' hut, which became a sanctuary to him.

At this point *Tarzan the Mighty* diverges from the canon. Ian McClosky Heath's original screen story shifts focus to a village, deep in the jungle, inhabited by an atavistic tribe of whites descended from pirates marooned on the African coast many generations before. The tribe is ruled by a shifty, opportunistic beachcomber named Black John (Ferguson), who has played on the superstitions of these ignorant people so long that they believe him possessed of near-supernatural powers.

Currently living among the tribe are Mary Trevor (Kingston) and her young brother Bobby (Nelson), castaways rescued by Black John and forced to accept his dubious hospitality. The erstwhile beachcomber has designs on the beautiful girl and hopes to make her his bride. That prospect repulses Mary, but she bides her time, hoping to keep Black John at arm's length long enough to arrange an escape.

The first episode ends on a thrilling note. While bathing in a jungle stream, Mary is imperiled by a monster crocodile. Her screams attract Tarzan, who's been swinging through the trees. The ape-man dives from great height into the water and grapples with the giant reptile as the chapter fades out.

Needless to say, the crocodile never lived that could clamp its jaws around Tarzan of the Apes, and Chapter Two opens with the jungle lord defeating the beast and making Mary's acquaintance. He rushes off to save one of his simian friends and the girl returns to the village, where Black John is already planning to trap her savior. In fact, he promises to give her Tarzan's head as a wedding present.

Hoping to lure the ape-man into his clutches, Black John prepares a trap for Tarzan's elephant friend, Tantor. Little Bobby, learning of the plot, dashes into the jungle to warn his new pal, only to be caught in Tantor's path when the terrified elephant is stampeded toward a spiked pit. Tarzan whisks Bobby into a nearby tree, but the limb breaks beneath their combined weight, plunging man and boy into the pit.

Chapter Three finds Tarzan dazed but unhurt by the fall; he and Bobby have narrowly missed the spikes embedded in the bottom of the pit. He brings the unconscious boy to his hut and attempts to revive him while Black John, claiming to have spirited Bobby away himself, bluffs Mary into consenting to marriage as

a means of having her brother restored to her. That night's wedding ceremony is disrupted by the unexpected arrival of Tarzan, who thrashes Black John in hand-to-hand combat but is surrounded and overcome by tribesmen. The episode draws to a close with the ape-man bound to a stake and Black John hurling a spear at him.

Subsequent chapters repeat the familiar serial pattern of capture and escape; Mary is forced several more times to participate in a marriage ceremony, but Tarzan always manages to rescue her before the vows can be exchanged. Eventually, Black John discovers that the ape-man is the scion of an English nobleman, and when the current Lord Greystoke (Lorimer Johnston) shows up looking for his long-lost relative, the crafty tribal chieftain uses papers stolen from Tarzan's hut to palm himself off as the missing heir. From this point forward, things get complicated.

Released nationally on August 13, 1928, *Tarzan the Mighty* was an instantaneous success. It was, in fact, a bonafide sensation. Serials were habitually ballyhooed to such an extent that they couldn't possibly measure up to studio hyperbole, but this one delivered the goods. Exhibitors reported standing-room-only crowds and record-breaking grosses. Having circulated a bare handful of episodes, Universal was besieged with requests to elongate the serial from 12 chapters to 15. This represented a significant change in attitude on the part of theater operators, who had bitterly complained just a few years earlier that Universal chapter plays—which at that time had a standard length of 18 installments—were padded with repetitious situations that bored patrons and caused them to abandon a serial halfway through. In 1926 the company settled on 10 chapters as the optimal length; since then only one serial—Blake of Scotland Yard—had gone longer, and by just two episodes at that.

Buoyed by exhibitor enthusiasm and thrilled with the prospect of squeezing additional revenue from *Tarzan the Mighty,* Laemmle ordered William Lord Wright to rework the serial's continuity and devise as many new situations as would be necessary to extend the chapter play by three installments. The decision was apparently made in mid-September, with principal photography already completed. It's not immediately clear from a reading of the synopses just where or how the storyline was stretched, although it's likely that Heath's shift of locale from the jungle to the high seas, and thence to England, was made during this chaotic period. By late October all 15 episodes had been completed, and the serial's playoff continued to the delight of exhibitors and patrons alike.

Universal was flooded with unsolicited endorsements, many of which made their way to the pages of Universal Weekly and into double-page advertisements placed in the leading trade journals. Typical of the raves was this one from Vogel Gettier, manager of the Capitol Theatre in Grand Island, Nebraska: "A box-office attraction and a real tonic for tired patrons. The only serial that has ever been booked in the Capitol, as it is the only one having real feature-picture strength. Pleases 100 percent all ages."

Said Ernest K. Pappas, manager of Copperfield, Utah's Diana Theatre: "Results and comments of patrons seeing Tarzan the Mighty were numerous, and all expressed satisfaction together with a promise to follow every episode to be shown. Box-office receipts on [opening day] surpassed every record for more than 16 months past."

"Tarzan the Mighty is the biggest attraction of its kind I've ever played," reported Roy W. Adams of Mason, Michigan's Pastime Theatre. "When the first and second episodes packed the house I thought it might be an accident—but it has held up consistently for six weeks now, doing two or three times as much business as any serial ever did in the past for me."

W. T. McEntyre, manager of the Princess Theatre is Enterprise, Alabama, declared: "I ran Chapter Eight last Saturday and did a tremendous business. My patrons say every episode gets better, and they are tickled to death that it has been extended to 15 episodes. It is the best serial I have ever run."

Such comments were printed not only in Universal advertisements but also in the avidly read "What the Picture Did for Me" column in *Exhibitors Herald,* which had recently merged with the venerable *Moving Picture World.*

An acquaintance of mine, the late Harold T. Penney, was nine years old when *Tarzan the Mighty* came to his local theater in Erie, Pennsylvania. Fifty years later, he still remembered it warmly. "Nothing like it ever came to town," he recalled for me in 1979. "You couldn't find an empty seat in the house on Saturday afternoon. We whooped and hol-

lered and carried on something awful when the main title flashed on screen. The noise was so loud you couldn't hardly hear the organ music. And after the show, we'd be walking home and climbing up every tree along the way, beating our chests and hanging off the limbs. We all wanted to be Tarzan. It's a wonder we didn't break our damn necks."

Viewers of all ages thrilled to Frank Merrill's feats of strength and agility. They marveled as he hauled himself up vines, hand over hand; as he swung from trees and darted through the jungle. They goggled at the shots of exotic beasts, some of which attacked each other in close-up while the camera rolled. It didn't seem to matter that the plot was thin and some of the chapter endings pedestrian. Everybody loved the serial; Universal reported that some exhibitors were running chapters two days a week instead of the usual one.

Tarzan the Mighty earned more in film rental—remember, that was the fee exhibitors paid to distributors, having nothing to do with box-office attendance— than any Universal movie released during 1928. That included such prestige feature-length attractions as Paul Fejos' *Lonesome* and Paul Leni's *The Man Who Laughs,* as well as the studio's enormously popular Reginald Denny comedies and Hoot Gibson Westerns. Edgar Rice Burroughs might not have been happy, but he was the only one who wasn't.

And what of Uncle Carl's relatives, the Stern brothers, whose 1922 purchase of the film rights to *Jungle Tales of Tarzan* had made all this possible? They were still gainfully employed at Universal, producing cheap two-reel comedy shorts. They did not participate financially in the serial's success; *Tarzan the Mighty's* huge profits went straight to Universal's bottom line. Julius and Abe knew they held a trump card, though: Laemmle would certainly want a sequel, but Burroughs was notoriously prickly when it came to dealing with Hollywood producers. And they still held the film rights to *Tarzan and the Jewels of Opar.*

That, however, is another story . . . .

ANTHONY TOLLIN

Tarzan, Lord of the Radio Jungle

Tarzan's mighty victory cry first erupted over the radio airwaves on September 5, 1932 as the syndicated *Tarzan of the Apes* debuted over St. Paul, Minnesota's KSTP, before expanding into wider syndication the following week. Often recognized as the first major syndicated adventure serial, the transcribed series eventually aired over some 60 stations. Former silent-screen Tarzan James Pierce enacted the title role, with Edgar Rice Burrough's daughter Joan co-starring as Jane Porter. The series' supporting cast included a number of future radio greats including Gale Gordon as Cecil Clayton, Jeanette Nolan as Princess La of Opar, Frank Nelson as Nikolas Rokoff and Hanley Stafford.

James Pierce had first portrayed Edgar Rice Burrough's legendary Jungle

Joan Burroughs Pierce and Jim Pierce on the set of *Tarzan and the Golden Lion.*

Lord in the 1927 silent screen serial, *Tarzan and the Golden Lion,* after being noticed by Tarzan's creator at a party at Burrough's ranch in Tarzana, California. "And then he proceeded to talk me into playing the Apeman," Pierce recalled. "He said I looked just like what he had always had in mind. . . . My salary as Tarzan was not much, but FPO assured me that it would skyrocket once I galloped cross the screen in a loincloth and the great American womanhood got a look at me. So with seventy-five dollars a week, I was off."

Pierce had previously been cast as an aviator in *Wings,* but quit the Paramount production to star as the Jungle Lord, with the young Gary Cooper taking over his role in what became the first Academy-Award-winning "Best Picture." The lukewarm reception of *Tarzan and the Golden Lion* almost ended Pierce's Hollywood career, but he came away with a great consulation prize. He began courting Joan Burroughs during the filming, and married ERB's only daughter on August 8, 1928.

Sponsor's advertisement plugging the Tarzan radio show.

Frederick C. Dahlquist's American Radio Features Syndicate produced 286 installments of the *Tarzan of the Apes* radio serial, the first 131 episodes based on ERB's first Tarzan novel and the final 155 installments adapted from *The Return of Tarzan.*

The Jungle Lord later returned to the airwaves in a pair of 39-chapter syndicated radio serials produced by Edgar Rice Burroughs, Inc., coordinated by ERB's son Hulbert Burroughs and Ralph Rothmund. Carlton Kadell enacted the title role in *Tarzan and the Diamond of Asher* (1934) and *Tarzan and the Fires of Tohr* (1936). John McIntire announced the serials, with Ralph Scott and Gale Gordon reprising their earlier roles as Paul D'Arnot and Cecil Clayton, and Jeanette Nolan and Barbara Luddy in supporting roles.

Gale Gordon and Joan Burroughs

Lamont Johnson voiced Tarzan when the Ape Man returned to the airwaves in a 1951 syndicated series from Walter White's Commodore Productions that later aired over CBS from March 22, 1952 through June 27, 1953. A former *Let's Pretend* cast member, Johnson achieved his greatest success as a director. The winner of four Director's Guild awards has directed 27 feature films and many acclaimed television productions including *Gore Vidal's Lincoln* and *Wallenberg* (starring Richard Chamberlain).

Jeanette Nolan (Princess La of Opar) at a microphone.

Edgar Rice Burroughs,
1916

O YOU KNOW TARZAN—Tarzan of the Apes? No more fascinating fiction-figure has ever been created than this white boy of noble birth who grows to manhood a wild thing among the wild things of the jungle. And it is therefore with the deepest pleasure that we present herewith the first of twelve stories of his adventures. These will appear exclusively in *The Blue Book Magazine,* one each month.

Tarzan's father and mother, you may remember, were Lord and Lady Greystoke, who were marooned by a mutinous ship's crew in the wilderness on the African coast. Soon afterward Lady Greystoke's baby was born; and for a year thereafter this little English family lived alone in their isolated jungle fastness, unable to escape and unable to find or summon succor. The story of their life was recorded by Greystoke—up to the time his wife died. And the next day, his vigilance relaxed in his grief, a troop of giant anthropoid apes attacked and killed him. A female of these jungle-folk had that day seen her own offspring dashed to death from a tree-top; and mother-instinct led her to snatch up the year-old child and carry it off with her. Soon "hunger closed the gap between them, and the son of an English lord and an English lady nursed at the breast of Kala, the great ape."

A part of the history of Tarzan has been chronicled, but many of his most striking adventures are yet to be told. A peculiar glamour gilds these captivating new stories—something of the bloom and radiance of the world's dawn glorifies Tarzan's life in the jungle; and you will find these wonder-tales uniquely refreshing. Moreover—but here comes Tarzan himself!

Editorial lead-in for ERB's new series, from *The Blue Book Magazine,* September 1916.

The New Stories of "TARZAN"

by Edgar Rice Burroughs

TEEKA, stretched at luxurious ease in the shade of the tropical forest, presented a most alluring picture of young feminine loveliness. At least, so thought Tarzan of the Apes, who squatted upon a low-swinging branch in a near-by tree and looked down upon her.

Just to have seen him there, lolling upon the swaying bough of the jungle-forest giant, his brown skin mottled by the brilliant equatorial sunlight which percolated through the leafy canopy of green above him, his clean-limbed body relaxed in graceful ease, his shapely head part turned in contemplative absorption and his intelligent gray eyes dreamily devouring the object of their devotion, you would have thought him the reincarnation of some demigod of old.

You would not have guessed that in infancy he had suckled at the breast of a hideous, hairy she-ape, nor that in all his conscious past since his parents had passed away in the little cabin by the land-locked harbor at the jungle's verge he had known no other associates than the sullen bulls and the snarling cows of the tribe of Kerchak, the great ape.

Editor's note: This story has been typeset from its appearance in the September 1916 issue of *The Blue Book Magazine,* allowing readers the opportunity to enjoy this work as Burroughs originally drafted it. Many of the subsequent book versions of his work were revised from their magazine appearances and appeared in somewhat altered forms.

Nor—could you have read the thoughts which passed through that active, healthy brain, the longings and desires and aspirations which the sight of Teeka inspired—would you have been any more inclined to give credence to the origin of the ape-man. For, from his thoughts alone, you could never have gleaned the truth—that he had been born to a gentle English lady or that his sire had been an English nobleman of honored lineage.

Lost to Tarzan of the Apes was the truth of his origin. That he was John Clayton, Lord Greystoke, with a seat in the House of Lords, he did not know; nor, knowing, would have understood.

Yes, Teeka was indeed beautiful! Of course Kala had been beautiful—one's mother is always that—but Teeka was beautiful in a way all her own, an indescribable sort of way which Tarzan was just beginning to sense rather vaguely.

For years had Tarzan and Teeka been playfellows, and Teeka still continued to be playful, while the young bulls of her own age were rapidly becoming surly and morose. Tarzan, if he gave the matter much thought at all, probably reasoned that his growing attachment for the young female could be easily accounted for by the fact that of the former playmates she and he alone retained any desire to frolic as of old.

But today, as he sat gazing upon her, he found himself noting the beauties of Teeka's form and features—something he had never done before, since none of them had aught to do with Teeka's ability to race nimbly through the lower terraces of the forest in the primitive games of tag and hide-and-go-seek which Tarzan's fertile brain evolved.

Tarzan scratched his head, running his fingers deep into the shock of black hair that framed his shapely boyish face. He scratched his head and sighed. Teeka's newfound beauty became as suddenly his despair. He envied her the handsome coat of hair that covered her body. His own smooth brown hide he hated with a hatred born of disgust and contempt. Years back, he had harbored a hope that some day he too would be clothed in hair, as were all his brothers and sisters; but of late he had been forced to abandon the delectable dream.

Then there were Teeka's great teeth, not so large as the male's, of course, but still mighty, handsome things by comparison with Tarzan's feeble white ones. And her beetling brows and broad, flat nose, and her mouth! Tarzan had often practiced making his mouth into a little round circle and then puffing out his cheeks while he winked his eyes rapidly; but he felt that he could never do it in the same cute and irresistible way in which Teeka did it.

And as he watched her that afternoon, and wondered, a young bull ape who had been lazily foraging for food beneath the damp, matted carpet of decaying vegetation at the roots of a near-by tree lumbered awkwardly in Teeka's direction. The other apes of the tribe of Kerchak moved listlessly about or lolled restfully in the midday heat of the equatorial jungle. From time to time one or another of them had passed close to Teeka, and Tarzan had been uninterested. Why was it, then, that his brows contracted and his muscles tensed as he saw Taug pause beside the young she and then squat down close to her?

Tarzan always had liked Taug. Since childhood they had romped together. Side by side had they squatted beside the water, their quick, strong fingers ready to leap forth and seize Pisah, the fish, should that wary denizen of the cool depths dart surfaceward to the lure of the insects Tarzan tossed upon the face of the pool.

Together they had baited Tublat and teased Numa, the lion. Why, then, should Tarzan feel the rise of the short hairs at the nape of his neck merely because Taug sat close to Teeka?

It is true that Taug was no longer the frolicsome ape of yesterday. When his snarling-muscles bared his giant fangs no one could longer imagine that Taug was in a playful mood as when he and Tarzan had rolled upon the turf in mimic battle. The Taug of today was a huge, sullen bull ape, somber and forbidding. Yet he and Tarzan never had quarreled.

For a few minutes the young apeman watched Taug press closer to Teeka. He saw the rough caress of the huge paw as it stroked the sleek shoulder of the she, and then Tarzan of the Apes slipped cat-like to the ground and approached the two.

As he came, his upper lip curled into a snarl, exposing his fighting fangs, and a deep growl rumbled from his cavernous chest. Taug looked up, batting his bloodshot eyes. Teeka half raised herself and looked at Tarzan. Did she guess the cause of his perturbation? Who may say? At any rate, she was feminine, and so she reached up and scratched Taug behind one of his small, flat ears.

Tarzan saw, and in that instant that he saw, Teeka was no longer the little playmate of an hour ago; instead she was a wondrous thing—the most wondrous in the world—and a possession for which Tarzan would fight to the death against Taug or any other who dared question his right of proprietorship.

Stooped, his muscles rigid and one great shoulder turned toward the young bull, Tarzan of the Apes sidled nearer and nearer. His face was partly averted, but his keen gray eyes never left those of Taug, and as he came his growls increased in depth and volume.

Taug rode upon his short legs, bristling. His fighting fangs were bared. He too sidled, stiff-legged, and growled.

"Teeka is Tarzan's," said the apeman in the low gutturals of the great anthropoids.

"Teeka is Taug's," replied the ape.

Thaka and Numgo and Gunto, disturbed by the growlings of the two young bulls, looked up, half apathetic, half interested. They were sleepy, but they sensed a fight. It would break the monotony of the humdrum jungle life they led.

Coiled about Tarzan's shoulders was a long grass rope; in his hand was the hunting knife of the long-dead father he had never known. In Taug's little brain lay a great respect for the shiny bit of sharp metal which the ape-boy knew so well how to use. With it had he slain Tublat, his fierce foster-father, and Bolgani, the gorilla. Taug knew these things, and so he came warily, circling about Tarzan in search of an opening. The latter, made cautious because of his lesser bulk and the inferiority of his natural armament, followed similar tactics.

For a time it seemed that the altercation would follow the way of the majority of such differences between members of the tribe, and that one of them would finally lose interest and wander off to prosecute some other line of endeavor. Such might have been the end of it had the *casus belli* been other than it was; but Teeka was flattered at the attention that was being drawn to her and by the fact that these two young bulls were contemplating battle on her account. Such a thing had never before occurred in Teeka's brief life. She had seen other bulls battling for other and older shes, and in the depth of her wild little heart she had longed for the day when the jungle grasses would be reddened with the blood of mortal combat for her fair sake.

So now she squatted upon her haunches and insulted both her admirers impartially. She hurled taunts at them for their cowardice, and called them vile names, such as, *"Histah,"* the snake, and *"Dango,"* the hyena. She threatened to call Mumga to chastise them with a stick—Mumga, who was so old that she could no longer climb and so toothless that she had to confine her diet almost exclusively to bananas and grub-worms.

The apes that were watching heard and laughed. Taug was infuriated. He made a sudden lunge for Tarzan, but the ape-boy leaped nimbly to one side, eluding him, and with the quickness of a cat wheeled and leaped back again to close quarters. His hunting knife was raised above his head as he came in, and he aimed a vicious blow at Taug's neck. The ape wheeled to dodge the weapon, so that the keen blade struck him but a glancing blow upon the shoulder.

The spurt of red blood brought a shrill cry of delight from Teeka. Ah, this was something worthwhile! She glanced about to see if others had witnessed this evidence of her popularity. Helen of Troy was never one whit more proud than was Teeka at that moment.

If Teeka had not been so absorbed her own vaingloriousness she might have noted the rustling of leaves in the tree above her—a rustling which was not caused by any movement of the wind, since there was no wind. And had she looked up, she might have seen a sleek body crouching almost directly over her and wicked yellow eyes glaring hungrily down upon her; but Teeka did not look up.

With his wound Taug had backed off, growling horribly. Tarzan followed him, screaming insults at him and menacing him with his brandishing blade. Teeka moved from beneath the tree in an effort to keep close to the duelists. Teeka had no intention of missing anything.

The branch above Teeka bent and swayed a trifle with the movement of the body of the watcher stretched along it. Taug had halted now and was preparing to make a new stand. His lips were flecked with foam, and saliva drooled from his jowls. He stood with head lowered and arms outstretched, preparing for a sudden charge to close quarters. Could he but lay his mighty hands upon that soft brown skin, the battle would be his. Taug considered Tarzan's manner of fighting unfair. He would not close. Instead he leaped nimbly just beyond the reach of Taug's muscular fingers.

The ape-boy had as yet never come to a real trial of strength with a bull ape, other than in play, and so he was not at all sure that it would be safe to put his muscles to the test in a life-and-death struggle. Not that he was afraid, for Tarzan knew nothing of fear; but the instinct of self-preservation gave him caution. He took risks only when it seemed necessary, and then he would hesitate at nothing.

His own method of fighting seemed best fitted to his build and to his armament His teeth, while strong and sharp, were, as weapons of offense, pitifully inadequate when compared with the mighty fighting fangs of the anthropoids. By dancing about just out of reach of an antagonist Tarzan could do infinite injury with his long, sharp hunting knife, and at the same time escape many of the painful and dangerous wounds that would be sure to follow his falling into the clutches of a bull ape.

And so Taug charged and bellowed like a bull, and Tarzan of the Apes danced lightly to this side and that, while he hurled jungle Billingsgate at his foe, and while he nicked him now and again with his knife.

There were lulls in the fighting when the two would stand panting for breath, facing each other, mustering their wits and their forces for a new onslaught. It was during a pause such as this that Taug chanced to let his eyes rove beyond his foeman. Instantly the entire aspect of the ape altered. Rage left his countenance, to be supplanted by an expression of fear.

With a cry that every ape there recognized Taug turned and fled. No need to question him: his warning proclaimed the near presence of their ancient enemy.

Tarzan started to seek safety, as did the other members of the tribe, and as he did so he heard a panther's scream mingled with the frightened cry of a she-ape. Taug heard too; but he did not pause in his flight.

With the ape-boy, however, it was different. He looked back to see if any member of the tribe was close pressed by the beast of prey, and the sight that met his eyes filled them with an expression of horror.

Teeka it was who cried out in terror as she fled across a little clearing toward the trees upon the opposite side, for after her leaped Sheeta, the panther, in easy, graceful bounds. Sheeta appeared to be in no hurry. His meat was assured, since even though the ape reached the trees ahead of him she could not climb beyond his clutches before he could be upon her.

Tarzan saw that Teeka must die. He cried to Taug and the other bulls to hasten to Teeka's assistance, and at the same time he ran toward the pursuing beast, taking down his rope as he came. Tarzan knew that once the great bulls were aroused, none of the jungle, not even Numa, the lion, was anxious to measure fangs with them, and that if all those of the tribe who chanced to be present today would charge, Sheeta, the great cat, would doubtless turn tail and run for his life.

Taug heard, as did the others; but no one came to Tarzan's assistance or Teeka's rescue, and Sheeta was rapidly closing up the distance between himself and his prey.

The ape-boy, leaping after the panther, cried aloud to the beast in an effort to turn it from Teeka or otherwise distract its attention until the she-ape could gain the safety of the higher branches where Sheeta dared not go. He called the panther every opprobrious name that fell to his tongue. He dared him to stop and do battle with him; but Sheeta only loped on after the luscious tidbit now almost within his reach.

Tarzan was not far behind, and he was gaining, but the distance was so short that he scarce hoped to overhaul the beast before it had felled Teeka. In his right hand the boy swung his grass rope above his head as he ran. He hated to chance a miss, for the distance was much greater than he had ever cast before except in practice. It was the full length of his grass rope that separated him from Sheeta, and yet there was no other thing to do. He could not reach the brute's side before it overhauled Teeka. He must chance a throw.

Just as Teeka sprang for the lower limbs of a great tree, and Sheeta rose behind her in a long, sinuous leap, the coils of the ape-boy's grass rope shot swiftly through the air, straightening into a long, thin line as the open noose hovered for an instant above the savage head and the snarling jaws. Then it settled—clean and true about the tawny neck it settled; and Tarzan, with a quick twist of his rope-hand, drew the noose taut, bracing himself for the shock when Sheeta should have taken up the slack.

Just short of Teeka's glossy haunches the cruel talons raked the air as the rope tightened, and Sheeta was brought to a sudden stop—a stop that snapped the big beast over upon his back. Instantly Sheeta was up—with glaring eyes and lashing tail and gaping jaws from which issued hideous cries of rage and disappointment.

He saw the ape-boy, the cause of his discomfiture, scarce forty feet before him, and Sheeta charged.

Teeka was safe now; Tarzan saw to that by a quick glance into the tree, the shelter of which she had gained not an instant too soon; and Sheeta was charging. It were useless to risk his life in idle and unequal combat from which no good could come; but could he escape a battle with the enraged cat? And if he was forced to fight, what chance had he to survive? Tarzan was constrained to admit that his position was aught but a desirable one. The trees were too far to hope to reach in time to elude the cat. Tarzan could but stand facing that hideous charge. In his right hand he grasped his hunting knife—a puny, futile thing indeed by comparison with the great rows of mighty teeth which lined Sheeta's powerful jaws, and the sharp talons encased within his padded paws; yet the young Lord Greystoke faced it with the same courageous resignation with which some fearless ancestor went down to defeat and death on Senlac Hill by Hastings.

From safety points in the trees the great apes watched, screaming hatred at Sheeta and advice at Tarzan, for the progenitors of man have, naturally, many human traits. Teeka was frightened. She screamed at the bulls to hasten to Tarzan's assistance; but the bulls were otherwise engaged—principally in giving advice and making faces. Anyway, Tarzan was not a real *mangani;* so why should they risk their lives in an effort to protect him?

And now Sheeta was almost upon the lithe, naked body, and—the body was not there. Quick as is the great cat, the ape-boy was quicker. He leaped to one side almost as the panther's talons were closing upon him, and as Sheeta went hurtling to the ground beyond, Tarzan was racing for the safety of the nearest tree.

The panther recovered itself almost immediately, and wheeling, tore after its prey, the ape-boy's rope dragging along the ground behind it. In doubling back after Tarzan, Sheeta had passed around a low bush. It was a mere nothing in the path of any jungle creature of the size and weight of Sheeta—provided the animal had no trailing rope dangling behind it. But Sheeta was handicapped by such a rope, and as he leaped once again after Tarzan of the Apes, the rope encircled the small bush, became tangled in it and brought the panther to a sudden stop. An instant later Tarzan was safe among the higher branches of a small tree into which Sheeta could not follow him.

Here he perched, hurling twigs and epithets at the raging feline beneath him. The other members of the tribe now took up the bombardment, using such hard-shelled fruits and dead branches as came within their reach, until Sheeta, goaded to frenzy and snapping at the grass rope, finally succeeded in severing its strands. For a moment the panther stood glaring first at one of his tormentors and then at another, until, with a final scream of rage, he turned and slunk off into the tangled mazes of the jungle.

A half-hour later the tribe was again upon the ground feeding as though naught had occurred to interrupt the somber dullness of their lives. Tarzan had recovered the greater part of his rope and was busy fashioning a new noose, while Teeka squatted close beside him, in evident token that her choice was made.

Taug eyed them sullenly. Once when he came close Teeka bared her fangs and growled at him, and Tarzan showed his canines in an ugly snarl; but Taug did not provoke a quarrel. He seemed to accept after the manner of his kind the decision of the she as an indication that he had been vanquished in his battle for her favors.

Later in the day, his rope repaired, Tarzan took to the trees in search of game. More than his fellows he required meat; and so, while they were satisfied with fruits and herbs and beetles, which could be discovered without considerable effort upon their parts, Tarzan spent considerable time hunting the game animals whose flesh alone satisfied the cravings of his stomach and furnished sustenance and strength to the mighty thews which, day by day, were building beneath the soft, smooth texture of his brown hide.

Taug saw him depart, and then, quite casually, the big beast hunted closer and closer to Teeka in his search for food. At last he was within a few feet of her, and when he shot a covert glance at her he saw that she was appraising him and that there was no evidence of anger upon her face.

Taug expanded his great chest and rolled about on his short legs, making strange growling noises in his throat. He raised his lips, baring his fangs. My, but what great, beautiful fangs he had! Teeka could not but notice them. She also let her eyes rest in admiration upon Taug's beetling brows and his short, powerful neck. What a beautiful creature he was indeed!

Taug, flattered by the unconcealed admiration in her eyes, strutted about, as proud and as vain as a peacock. Presently he commenced to inventory his assets, mentally, and shortly he found himself comparing them with those of his rival.

Taug grunted, for there was no comparison. How could one compare his beautiful coat with the smooth and naked hideousness of Tarzan's bare hide? Who could see beauty in the stingy nose of the *tarmangani* after looking at Taug's broad nostrils? And Tarzan's eyes! Hideous things, showing white about them, and entirely unrimmed with red! Taug knew that his own bloodshot eyes were beautiful, for he had seen them reflected in the glassy surface of many a drinking-pool.

The bull drew closer to Teeka, finally squatting close against her. When Tarzan returned from his hunting a short time later, it was to see Teeka contentedly scratching the back of his rival.

Tarzan was disgusted. Neither Taug nor Teeka saw him as he swung through the trees into the glade. He paused a moment looking at them; then, with a sorrowful grimace, he turned and faded away into the labyrinth of leafy boughs and festooned moss out of which he had come.

Tarzan wished to be as far away from the cause of his heartache as he could. He was suffering the first pangs of blighted love, and he didn't quite know what was the matter with him. He thought that he was angry with Taug, and so he couldn't understand why it was that he had run away instead of rushing into mortal combat with the destroyer of his happiness.

He also thought that he was angry with Teeka; yet a vision of her many beauties persisted in haunting him, so that he could only see her in the light of love as the most desirable thing in the world.

The ape-boy craved affection. From babyhood until the time of her death, when the poisoned arrow of Kulonga had pierced her savage heart, Kala had represented to the English boy the sole object of love that he had known.

In her wild, fierce way, Kala had loved her adopted son; and Tarzan had returned that love, though the outward demonstrations of it were no greater than might have been expected from any other beast of the jungle. It was not until he was bereft of her that the boy realized how deep had been his attachment for his mother, for as such he looked upon her.

In Teeka he had seen within the past few hours a substitute for Kala—someone to fight for and to hunt for—someone to caress; but now his dream was shattered. Something hurt within his breast. He placed his hand over his heart and wondered what had happened to him. Vaguely he attributed his pain to Teeka. The more he thought of Teeka as he had last seen her, caressing Taug, the more the thing within his breast hurt him.

Tarzan shook his head and growled; then on and on through the jungle he swung, and the farther he traveled and the more he thought upon his wrongs, the nearer he approached becoming an irreclaimable misogynist.

* * * * *

Two days later he was still hunting alone—very morose and very unhappy; but he was determined never to return to the tribe. He could not bear the thought of seeing Taug and Teeka always together. As he swung upon a great limb Numa the lion and Sabor the lioness passed beneath him, side by side, and Sabor leaned against the lion and bit playfully at his cheek. It was a half-caress. Tarzan sighed and hurled a nut at them.

Later Tarzan came upon several of Mbonga's black warriors. He was upon the point of dropping his noose about the neck of one of them who was a little distance from his companions when he became interested in the thing that occupied the savages. They were building a cage in the trail and covering it with leafy branches. When they had completed their work, the structure was scarcely visible.

Tarzan wondered what the purpose of the thing might be—and why, when they had built it, they turned away and started back along the trail in the direction of their village.

It had been some time since Tarzan had visited the blacks and looked down from the shelter of the great tree that overhung their palisade upon the activities of his enemies—from among whom had come the slayer of Kala.

Although he hated them, Tarzan derived considerable entertainment in watching them at their daily life within their village, and especially at their dances, when the fires glared against their naked bodies as they leaped and turned and twisted in mimic warfare. It was rather in the hope of witnessing something of the kind that he now followed the warriors back toward their village, but in this he was disappointed, for there was no dance that night.

Instead, from the safe concealment of his tree, Tarzan saw little groups seated about tiny fires discussing the events of the day, and in the darker corners of the village he descried isolated couples talking and laughing together; and always one of each couple was a young man and the other a young woman.

Tarzan cocked his head upon one side and thought, and before he went to sleep that night, curled in the crotch of the great tree above the village, Teeka filled his mind; and afterward she filled his dreams—she and the young black men laughing and talking with the young black women.

Taug, hunting alone, had wandered a considerable distance from the balance of the tribe. He was making his way slowly along an elephant path when he discovered that it was blocked with undergrowth. Now Taug, come into maturity, was an evil-natured brute of an exceeding short temper. When something thwarted him, his sole idea was to overcome it by brute strength and ferocity, and so now when he found his way blocked, he tore angrily into the leafy screen—and an instant later found himself within a strange lair, his progress effectually blocked notwithstanding his most violent efforts to forge ahead

Biting and striking at the barrier, Taug finally worked himself into a frightful rage; but all to no avail, and at last he became convinced that he must turn back; but when he would have done so, what was his chagrin to discover that another barrier had dropped behind him while he fought to break down the one before him. Taug was trapped. Until exhaustion overcame him he fought frantically for his freedom, but all to no avail.

In the morning a party of blacks set out from the village of Mbonga in the direction of the trap they had constructed the previous day, while among the branches of the trees above them hovered a naked young giant filled with the curiosity of the wild thing. Manu, the monkey, chattered and scolded as Tarzan passed, and though he was not afraid of the familiar figure of the ape-boy, he hugged closer to him the little brown body of his life's companion. Tarzan laughed as he saw it; but the laugh was followed by a sudden clouding of his face and a deep sigh.

A little farther on, a gaily-feathered bird strutted about before the admiring eyes of his somber-hued mate. It seemed to Tarzan that everything in the jungle was combining to remind him that he had lost Teeka; yet every day of his life he had seen these same things and thought nothing of them.

When the blacks reached the trap, Taug set up a great commotion. Seizing the bars of his prison, he shook them frantically, and all the while he roared and growled terrifically. The blacks were elated, for while they had not built their trap for this hairy tree-man, they were delighted with their catch.

Tarzan pricked up his ears when he heard the voice of a great ape, and circling quickly until he was down-wind from the trap, he sniffed at the air in search of the scent-spoor of the prisoner. Nor was it long before there came to those delicate nostrils the familiar odor that told Tarzan the identity of the captive as unerringly as though he had looked upon Taug with his eyes. Yes, it was Taug, and he was alone.

Tarzan grinned as he approached to discover what the blacks would do to their prisoner. Doubtless they would slay him at once. Again Tarzan grinned. Now he could have Teeka for his own, with none to dispute his right to her. As he watched, he saw the black warriors strip the screen from about the cage, fasten the ropes to it and drag it away along the trail in the direction of their village.

Tarzan watched until his rival passed out of sight, still beating upon the bars of his prison and growling out his anger and his threats; then the ape-boy turned and swung rapidly off in search of the tribe and Teeka.

Once, upon the journey, he surprised Sheeta and his family in a little overgrown clearing. The great cat lay stretched upon the ground, while his mate, one paw across her lord's savage face, licked at the soft white fur at his throat.

Tarzan increased his speed then until he fairly flew through the forest; nor was it long before he came upon the tribe. He saw them before they saw him, for of all the jungle creatures, none passed more quietly than Tarzan of the Apes. He saw Kamma and her mate feeding side by side, their hairy bodies rubbing against one another. And he saw Teeka feeding by herself. Not for long would she feed thus in loneliness, thought Tarzan, as with a bound he landed amongst them.

There was a startled rush and a chorus of angry and frightened snarls, for Tarzan had surprised them; but there was more, too, than mere nervous shock to account for the bristling neckhair that remained standing long after the apes had discovered the identity of the newcomer.

Tarzan noticed this as he had noticed it many times in the past—that always his sudden coming among them left them nervous and unstrung for a considerable time, and that they one and all found it necessary to satisfy themselves that he was indeed Tarzan by smelling about him half a dozen or more times before they calmed down.

Pushing through them, he made his way toward Teeka; but as he approached her, the ape drew away, baring her teeth in a snarl of fear.

"Teeka," he said, "it is Tarzan. You belong to Tarzan. I have come for you."

The ape drew closer, looking him over carefully. Finally she sniffed at him, as though to make assurance doubly sure.

"Where is Taug?" she asked.

"The *gomangani* have him," replied Tarzan. "They will kill him."

In the eyes of the she, Tarzan saw a wistful expression and a troubled look of sorrow as he told her of Taug's fate; but she came quite close and snuggled against him, and Tarzan, Lord Greystoke, put his arm about her.

As he did so, he noticed with a start the strange incongruity of that smooth, brown arm against the black and hairy coat of his lady-love. He recalled the paw of Sheeta's mate across Sheeta's face—no incongruity there. He thought of little Manu hugging his mate, and how the one seemed to belong to the other. Even the proud male bird with his gay plumage bore a close resemblance to his quieter spouse, while Numa, but for his shaggy mane, was almost a counterpart of the lioness Sabor. The males and females differed, it was true; but not with such difference as existed between Tarzan and Teeka.

Tarzan was puzzled. There was something wrong. His arm dropped from the shoulder of Teeka. Very slowly he drew away from her. She looked at him with her head cocked upon one side. Tarzan rose to his full height and beat upon his breast with his fists. He raised his head toward the heavens and opened his mouth. From the depths of his lungs rose the fierce, weird challenge of the victorious bull ape. The tribe turned curiously to eye him. He had killed nothing; nor was there any antagonist to be goaded to madness by the savage scream. No, there was no excuse for it, and they turned back to their feeding, but with an eye upon the ape-man lest he be preparing to run suddenly amuck.

As they watched him, they saw him swing into a near-by tree and disappear from sight. Then they forgot him, even Teeka.

Mbonga's black warriors, sweating beneath their strenuous task, and resting often, made slow progress toward their village. Always the savage beast in the primitive cage growled and roared when they moved him. He beat upon the bars and slavered at the mouth. His noise was hideous.

They had almost completed their journey and were taking their final rest before forging ahead to gain the clearing in which lay their village. A few more minutes would have taken them out of the forest, and then, doubtless, the thing would not have happened which did happen.

A silent figure moved through the trees above them. Keen eyes inspected the cage and counted the number of the warriors. An alert and daring brain figured upon the chances of success when a certain plan should be put to the test.

Tarzan watched the blacks lolling in the shade. They were exhausted. Already several of them slept. He crept closer, pausing just above them. Not a leaf rustled before his stealthy advance. He waited in the infinite patience of the beast of prey. Presently but two of the warriors remained awake, and one of these was dozing. It was not long before his head nodded upon his breast.

Tarzan of the Apes gathered himself, and as he did so, the black that did not sleep arose and passed around to the rear of the cage. The ape-boy followed just above his head. Taug was eying the warrior and emitting low growls. Tarzan feared the anthropoid would awaken the sleepers.

In a whisper that was inaudible to the ears of the Negro, Tarzan whispered Taug's name, cautioning the ape to silence, and Taug's growling ceased.

The black approached the rear of the cage and examined the fastenings of the door, and as he stood there, Tarzan above him threw himself from the tree full upon the man's back. Steel fingers circled the black's throat, choking the cry that sprang to his lips. Strong teeth fastened themselves in his shoulder, and powerful legs around themselves in an unshakable grip about his torso.

The black in a frenzy of terror tried to dislodge the silent thing that clung to him. He threw himself to the ground and rolled about; but still those mighty fingers closed more and more tightly in their deadly grip.

The man's mouth gaped wide; his swollen tongue protruded; his eyes started from their sockets: but the relentless fingers only increased their pressure.

Taug was silent witness of the struggle. In his fierce little brain he doubtless wondered what purpose prompted Tarzan to attack the black. Taug had not forgotten his recent battle with the ape-boy, or the cause of it. Now he saw the form of the *gomangani* go suddenly limp. There was a convulsive shiver, and after a moment the man lay still.

Tarzan sprang from his prey and ran to the door of the cage. With nimble fingers he worked rapidly at the thongs that held the door in place. Taug could only watch—he could not help. Presently Tarzan pushed the thing up a couple of feet, and Taug crawled out. The ape would have turned upon the sleeping blacks, that he might wreak his pent-up vengeance; but Tarzan would not permit it.

Instead, the ape-boy dragged the body of the black within the cage and propped it against the side bars. Then he lowered the door and made fast the thongs as they had been before.

A happy smile lighted his features as he worked, for one of his principal diversions was the baiting of the blacks of Mbonga's village. He could imagine their terror when they awoke and found the dead body of their comrade fast in the cage where they had left the great ape safely secured but a few minutes before.

Tarzan and Taug took to the trees together, the shaggy coat of the fierce ape brushing the sleek skin of the English lordling as they passed through the primeval jungle side by side.

"Go back to Teeka," said Tarzan. "She is yours. Tarzan does not want her."

"Tarzan has found another she?" asked Taug.

The ape-boy shrugged.

"For the *gomangani* there is another *gomangani,*" he said; "for Numa the lion there is Sabor the lioness; for Sheeta there is a she of his own kind; for Bara the deer, for Manu the monkey, for all the beasts and the birds of the jungle is there a mate. Only for Tarzan of the Apes is there none. Taug is an ape. Teeka is an ape. Go back to Teeka. Tarzan is a man. He will go alone."

• • • • •

Tarzan at MGM

Any celebration of the work of Edgar Rice Burroughs would be incomplete without some reference to Johnny Weissmuller. Here are two publicity stills for *Tarzan the Ape Man,* released in March 1932 with Weismuller and Maureen O'Sullivan.

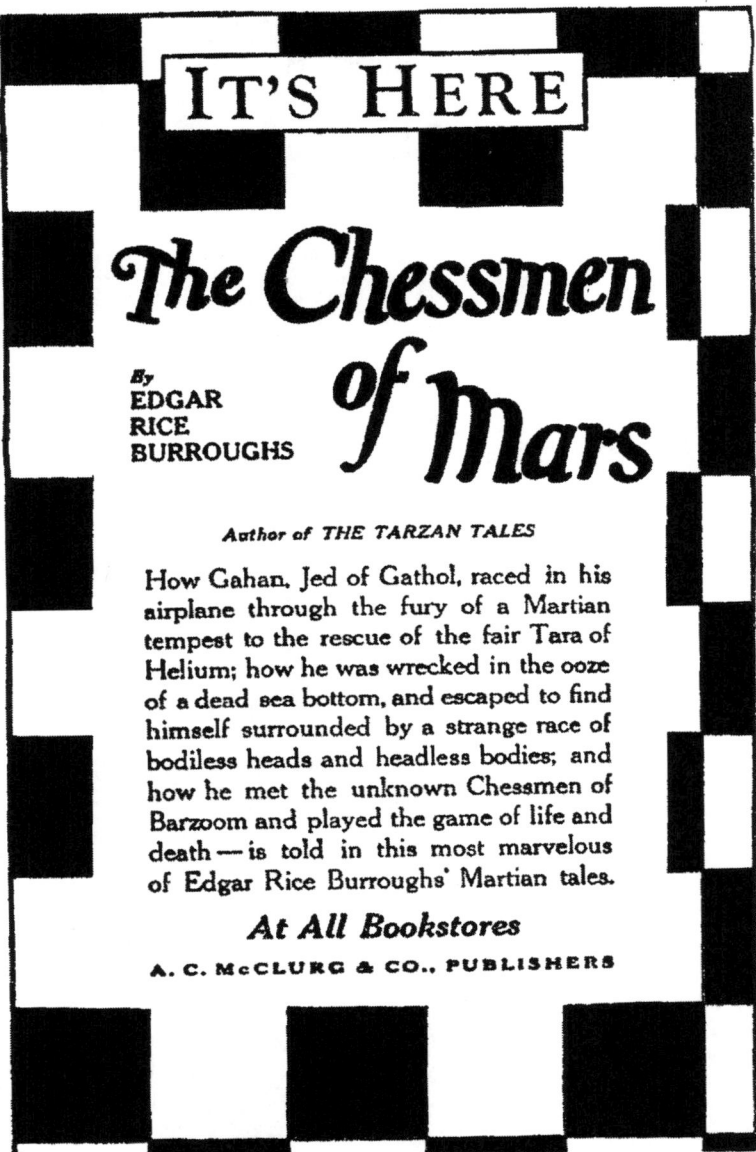

IT'S HERE

The Chessmen of Mars

By EDGAR RICE BURROUGHS

Author of THE TARZAN TALES

How Gahan, Jed of Gathol, raced in his airplane through the fury of a Martian tempest to the rescue of the fair Tara of Helium; how he was wrecked in the ooze of a dead sea bottom, and escaped to find himself surrounded by a strange race of bodiless heads and headless bodies; and how he met the unknown Chessmen of Barzoom and played the game of life and death — is told in this most marvelous of Edgar Rice Burroughs' Martian tales.

At All Bookstores

A. C. McCLURG & CO., PUBLISHERS

The Boston Globe, December 16, 1922

LEIGH BRACKETT

Barsoom and Myself

Statistically, I was born in Los Angeles a sufficient number of years ago, and I was fortunate enough to spend most of my childhood on a California beach, before the marinas and subdividers came. There, before fishing and swimming and the inevitable school-going, I came by some stroke of fate upon *The Gods of Mars*. My age was, I think, around eight years. There was a fanfare of trumpets, a celestial curtain rose and a great light shone upon me, and I was never the same again. Mars became my second home, and I think I lived there almost as much as I did in Venice, Cal. This kind of thing caused my elders much pain and they tried to wean me away from such foolishness, but it didn't work and they finally gave up. (I don't mean to give the impression that I became totally dedicated to science fiction. I didn't. We had lively wrangles over the other things I read, as well . . . all about pirates and Indians and wild animals and such. I loved them all. It was just that other worlds, and especially Mars, had a magic for me that was different from everything else.)

I started to scribble words on little pieces of paper when I was around eight. They were not science fiction stories. I think that was too big, somehow too sacred, for me to play with. I wrote instead a long sequel to *The Mark of Zorro*. Later, when I decided formally at the age of 13 to become a writer, I turned to more contemporary themes. The results were remarkable, but not saleable! I tried my hand at this and that, but it wasn't until I made up my mind that science fiction was what I wanted to write that I began to make any headway.

The headway came about through another stroke of fate . . . the meeting with Henry Kuttner, who was then reading (in his spare time, though God knows how he had any, considering the wordage he was turning out) for a literary agency. Far above and beyond the call of duty, Henry read, re-read, criticized, and all but re-wrote my limping efforts until finally one day they sold, and I had in fact become a writer. Blessed be his memory!

And now I too could write stories about Mars. And did. And I think that no one who has read both Burroughs and Brackett could doubt for a moment that Brackett's Mars grew root and branch out of Burroughs. The dead cities beneath the hurtling moons of Barsoom, the dead sea-bottoms, the feeling of ancientness and vanished glory. . . these were all stamped so powerfully on my mind that I could not possibly have written about, or conceived of any other Mars. I like to think that I did not copy . . . that there was enough of the individual Brackett woven into the concept to make my own Mars indeed my own. But the inspiration was clear enough.

This article first appeared in *ERBania*, no.19, 1966, and is reprinted by permission of the publisher Peter Ogden.

$\mathcal{B}$ARSOOM

"Edgar Rice Burroughs influenced me more than any other single author."
—Leigh Brackett

Roy Krenkel

And let me say now that Mars is still my favorite planet. I have written suspense novels, and westerns, and some mainstream pieces, and each one has its own special appeal and I love them and enjoy writing them. But not in the same way I love Mars. When I was eight or nine I used to go outside at night and stand on the cold sand with the sea-wind blowing, and stretch my arms up to Mars, hoping like John Carter to be translated to the Red Planet in the twinkling of an eye. It never happened, probably fortunately for me, not being a great swordsman and hardly able at that age (or at this one, either!) to cope with great white apes or bloodthirsty Tharks. But the thought was there, and I don't recall ever having the same urge to be transported to any other place or time, though I've always been fascinated by the history, especially the ancient history, of this planet.

It is always difficult to sort out, in later years, exactly what influences pushed one this way or that, because so many of them are subconscious. But one thing is very certain. Edgar Rice Burroughs influenced me more than any other single author, and that is saying one whale of a lot, considering how much I was influenced in those same plastic, impressionable years, by other idols—Rudyard Kipling, Rider Haggard, Jack London.

I believe that because of Burroughs I became a writer of a certain type cf science fiction; possibly it was because of Burroughs that I became a science fiction writer at all, and it is possibly because of science fiction that I became a writer at all. And it does my heart good to see the newsstands loaded with ERB, just going to prove that if you can tell a real story your tales will outlive all the John Galsworthy's in the world, regardless of how the lady librarians may sneer at them.

· · · · ·

Burroughs is probably the most influential writer in the entire history of the world.
—Ray Bradbury

Congratulations to
2011 Munsey Award Winner
Anthony Tollin

Photo courtesy Michael Piper

I am honored to win the second annual Munsey Award, named in honor of the man whose legendary magazines introduced John Carter and Tarzan, and who was eulogized as contributing "to the journalism of his day the talent of a meat packer, the morals of a money changer and the manner of an undertaker." I am humbled to be part of such a glorious tradition!

Thanks to those who voted for me, and to the committees of both Pulpfest and the Windy City Pulp and Paperback Convention for their tireless work to provide wonderful venues for enthusiasts to share their love of pulp fiction. I will continue to do all I can to preserve and publicize the fantastic fiction of decades past, and the memories of the talented writers, editors and artists who created that literary magic.

Anthony Tollin

In addition to his skills as a writer and historian, Anthony Tollin as a longtime DC Comics employee participated in the comic book revivals of Tarzan, Korak, The Shadow, Justice, Inc., John Carter, Carson of Venus and Doc Savage, and in 1979 co-authored *The Shadow Scrapbook* with Walter B. Gibson. As the editor-publisher of Sanctum Books, Anthony has issued 122 Shadow novels and hopes to eventually bring all 325 Shadow pulp novels back into print in uniform editions. He has also published authorized editions of 120 Doc Savage novels, plus reprints of The Avenger and The Whisperer.

During his decade-long association with Radio Spirits, Anthony Tollin wrote more than 70 historical booklets for OTR cassette and CD releases, including many collections of pulp-related radio programs that further promoted this bygone era, and helped introduce its classic characters to new generations of fans. He also scripted more than a thousand episodes of the nationally syndicated *When Radio Was* hosted by Stan Freberg and two historical scripts narrated by Walter Cronkite, and also served as Historical Consultant on the television documentary *Martian Mania: the True Story of the War of the Worlds* hosted by James Cameron.

105

From Pulp to the Silver Screen, 2012

In conjunction with our convention theme, this year's film program celebrates the 100th anniversary of Edgar Rice Burroughs' first published stories, which appeared in Frank A. Munsey's classic pulp, *The All-Story Magazine*. ERB's initial contribution, "Under the Moons of Mars" (later published in hardcover as *A Princess of Mars),* introduced John Carter, who finally reached the big screen this year. But it was the publication of "Tarzan of the Apes," complete in *All-Story's* October 1912 issue, that assured Edgar's place in pop-culture history. Therefore, the ape-man appears in most of our films this weekend—but we've included a brace of non-Tarzan movies for variety.

Friday—

12:00PM
Tarzan and the Tiger (1929)
(Chapters 1-7)

Don't let the idiotic title fool you: this 15-chapter serial is a reasonably faithful adaptation of *Tarzan and the Jewels of Opar,* ERB's fifth novel featuring the ape-man. Filmed at the tail end of the silent-movie era, it was released to theaters with a sound track of music and sound effects, including the first cinematic version of Tarzan's victory cry. Gymnastic champion Frank Merrill stars as Lord Greystoke and beautiful Natalie Kingston plays his Lady Jane. The exotic actress/dancer Mademoiselle Kithnou makes a sensual La of Opar, and the villainy is essayed by Al Ferguson, Sheldon Lewis and Paul Panzer—veteran serial heavies all. Our print of the complete chapter play is tinted and toned, and it has the original 1929 sound track.

2:00PM
The Lion Man (1936)

Loosely adapted from ERB's 1917 *All-Story Weekly* serial "The Lad and the Lion," this Poverty Row production stars Charles Locher (soon to achieve limited stardom as Jon Hall) as El Lion, aka Ronald Chatham. The son of an English mineralogist, he survives an Arab massacre and grows up with a holy man who teaches him to live among lions. *The Lion Man* takes little from its source except basic premise and general setting, but it's a fascinating "B" picture nonetheless. Kathleen Burke, the erstwhile "Panther Woman" of Paramount's *The Island of Lost Souls* (1933), has the leading female role.

Jon Hall stars as El Lion, *The Lion Man* (1936)

3:15PM
Tarzan and the Tiger (1929)
(Chapters 8-15)

Post-Auction:
Tarzan and the Golden Lion (1927)

This silent-movie version of ERB's 1922 novel (serialized in *Argosy All-Story Weekly* before seeing print in book form) adheres in general outlines to the original yarn but falls somewhat short in the thrills department. Upon initial theatrical release it proved disappointing to both critics and customers, and was the least financially successful Tarzan movie up to that point. However, it remains of historical interest for several reasons, including the title-role casting of James Pierce (who fell in love with and eventually married ERB's daughter Joan) and the appearance of a pre-*Frankenstein* Boris Karloff as a witch doctor. Long thought lost, the film turned up in a foreign archive some years ago. The version we're showing restores the original English-language intertitles, is tinted and toned, and sports a musical track.

Saturday—

9:00AM
Tarzan and His Mate (1934)

Although our lineups are usually confined to films adapted from pulp stories, we realized there was no way we could salute ERB's immortal ape man without including one of Johnny Weissmuller's Tarzan movies. And this one is far and away the best of the bunch. The second in M-G-M's series, *Mate* continues the first film's search for the legendary Elephant's Graveyard. But Harry Holt (played by Neil Hamilton) isn't just after a fortune in ivory: he also plans on persuading Jane Parker (Maureen O' Sullivan) to leave Tarzan and return to England with him. The action scenes—including the ape man's classic tussle with a giant crocodile—are first rate, but *Mate* also commands interest as the most erotically charged of M-G-M's Tarzan films.

11:00AM
The Son of Tarzan (1920)
(Sample chapters)

Another faithful ERB adaptation, with the early episodes (which we're showing) following the 1915 *All-Story* version almost scene for scene. Kamuela Searle stars as Korak the Killer and P. Dempsey Tabler plays Tarzan. Over a period of several decades this rare serial held a special fascination for fans owing to a report that Hawaii-born Searle had died from injuries sustained during the filming of the last chapter and was replaced by a double in the closing scenes. This story, recounted in Gabe Essoe's 1968 book *Tarzan of the Movies* and repeated in several sources after that, has since been debunked: Searle *was* doubled in a couple shots but made a full recovery and appeared in one more motion picture before quitting the business in 1921 to become an artist and sculptor.

12:30PM
Tarzan: Lord of the Louisiana Jungle (2011) Documentary
The first film to feature ERB's immortal ape man, *Tarzan of the Apes* (1918), was mainly shot in and around Morgan City, Louisiana. The densely foliated bayou country impressed producer William Parsons as being an acceptable simulacrum of the African jungle, so he shipped cast, crew and animals to the Pelican State for shooting of exterior scenes. This documentary, made by executive producer Al Bohl in partnership with the award-winning Cinematic Arts Workshop of the University of Louisiana, chronicles the production of that 1918 classic and reveals much information thought lost to history.

2:00PM
Tarzan of the Apes (1918)
You'll want to see the original movie with the documentary fresh in your mind. Originally released at a length of 12 reels (over two hours in running time), the film was subsequently cut, and cut again, for theatrical reissues and 16mm versions aimed at the non-theatrical market. This 61-minute version captures all the highlights. You'll see barrel-chested Elmo Lincoln in the role that made him an international star (and which he revisited twice, first in a 1918 sequel, *The Romance of Tarzan*, and then in a 1921 serial, *The Adventures of Tarzan*).

Elmo Lincoln in his first outing as Tarzan,

3:00PM
At the Earth's Core (1976)

A follow-up to 1975's *The Land That Time Forgot*, this lively adaptation of ERB's first Pellucidar novel remains a favorite of baby boomers who saw it theatrically. Doug McClure (from TV's *The Virginian*) stars as David Innes, with Hammer horror-movie favorites Peter Cushing and Caroline Munro as Abner Perry and Dian respectively. The special effects are a bit on the cheesy side, some of the acting is over the top, and on the whole the film is too ambitious for its obviously modest production mounting, but *At the Earth's Core* remains a lot of fun. We predict it'll bring back fond memories to those of you who caught it during a Saturday matinee or on a drive-in double bill.

4:30PM
Tarzan the Fearless (1933)

In the interest of representing as many screen Tarzans as possible, we're including this feature-length cutdown of Sol Lesser's 12-chapter serial starring Buster Crabbe as ERB's apeman. Produced the year after M-G-M's first Weissmuller Tarzan, *Fearless* was the result of a grand compromise between Burroughs and Lesser, who had obtained limited rights to the character from people who had licensed them several years earlier. Although Lesser could have exercised his option immediately, he agreed to hold off at ERB's request. Doing so worked to his benefit, as the success of Metro's first Weissmuller entry reinvigorated moviegoers' interest in Tarzan and facilitated the marketing of Lesser's most modest production.

Post-Auction:
Tarzan and the Green Goddess (1935)

A few years back we ran the first of two feature films edited down from the serial produced by ERB himself, *The New Adventures of Tarzan*. This year we're screening the second, which is arguably the more interesting of the two because it includes a substantial amount of footage not shot for the chapter play. (You can identify the previously unused footage easily because in those scenes leading lady Ula Holt wears a dark blouse, as opposed to the khaki top she wore in the serial.) Largely shot on location in Guatemala, where the story takes place, *Green Goddess* stars 1928 Olympic champion Herman Brix as Tarzan, who for the first time in a talking picture is played as Burroughs wrote him.

MURANIA
PRESS

Selected Verse

"Under the Moons of Mars" was not the first use by Edgar Rice Burroughs of the nom de plume "Normal Bean." Burroughs had at least eight pieces of verse appear in the *Chicago Tribune* between October 1910 and May 1915 under that byline.

Must Fight or Run Out

They say that Rome began to rot,
    And took the count, and went to pot
Because the gladiator kids
    Caved in each other's bloomin' lids.
These same highbrows likewise opine
    That fighting bulls caused Spain's decline.
And when two gents pull off a scrap
    They stand upon their ears and yap.
And pull their whiskers out and shriek:
    "The Ship of State has sprang a leak."
If I were but a mental coot
    I might their arguments refute.
I'd make a bow, and tip my hat.
    And gracefully remind them that
The fact that Caesar loved a scrap
    Was what put Rome upon the map:
And Spanish slaves did Moorish will
    Till Spaniards learned to fight to kill.
I'd hate to see this land all pug's,
    Or mental gents, or baseball bug's;
But some of each helps on the rest,
    Provided each bloke does his best.
To those who say the fighter's worst
    I might remark: "He's also first.
Because some ancient guy could fight
    You owe the fact you're here tonight.

Normal Bean, *Chicago Tribune,* October 15, 1910
Picked up and reprinted in *The Brownsville Herald,* (Brownsville, Texas) October 21, 1910

Nay, It Hath Not Gone

Oh, who hath copped the Wailing Place
    I ask you, dear old pal.
No Place they keep where one may weep
    In sunny southern Cal.
The butcher man he robs me blind;
    Robs me the grocer deft;
The brigand cruel who sells me fuel
    He taketh what is left.
The garage man (accent the gar),
    Unmindful of my groans,
He wrecks my car with loud Har! Har!
    And later picks my bones.
And now the Wailing Place is gone
    Where shall we find us rest?
Unless you say: "Come hither pray,
    And weep upon my vest."

Normal Bean, *Chicago Tribune,* February 3, 1914

The Contribs of Yesterday

From out the yellow, musty past
    Of faded files and drear
I wriggle from oblivion
    To answer, "Master, here!"

My old blood starts and almost flows—
    Ah, memory sublime!—
Of long gone day when first I made—
    (Aw, shucks! that doesn't rime.)

Yet once again before I go
    To reap reward condign
I'm glad that I have heard the call—
    The old call of the line;

The call that's old, yet ever young,
    Nor time, nor age can stint:
The ancient call for which I fall—
    To see my name in print.

Normal Bean, *Chicago Tribune,* May 31, 1915

Newspaper advertisement selling stock in the National Film Corporation of America
Oak Leaves (Oak Park, Illinois) August 12, 1916

EDGAR RICE BURROUGHS

Will Go Gypsying All Summer

*Oak Park Man to Take His Household for a Unique Automobile Trip
to Nowhere in Particular—Will Break the Procrastination Record*

My friend Otto McFeely, having successfully kidded himself into the belief that there is something interesting in plans I am making for a camping trip this summer, obtained my promise, during a moment of mental aberration, to inflict upon you an account of something which cannot possibly interest anyone other than my family and myself.

A harrowing detail of the transaction lies in the fact that I am to receive nothing per word for my labor, and that when I finally—and tearfully—view it in print it may be so horribly pock-marked with simp spelling as to be unrecognizable; but that is another harrow.

Among other things to which "the so called human race" is heir nothing is more prevalent in Spring than wanderlust. You have it, I have it, we all have it; but I have it worst, for I have it constantly from January 1 to December 31. It is contagious, too. I know it, for my wife, who was formerly a very domestic sort of person, is now quite as bad as I. In sixteen years we have moved sixteen times and lived in seven different towns—absolutely disproving the theory that it is cheaper to move than pay rent.

Of course "really nice people" don't do such things; but we can't all be nice.

And now, this summer, we are going to solve the problem by keeping on the move continually. We are going on what one might call a Gypsy tour, were one, like Mr. McFeely, poetic.

We—that stands for the whole family, and, true to Oak Park ideals, it is some family, in which there lurks no slightest taint of race suicide—we, as I started to say, have bought a tent and are going camping.

How's that for literary art? I have said in some two hundred and fifty words, at nothing per word, what I might have said in four—we are going camping. That is about all there is to it, so you might as well turn back to the obituaries and church news. But if you at all resemble the poetic Otto you will see such possibilities in those four words that you will be enthralled—as was he, and as we are.

Our equipment consists of one 12x20, three-room compartment tent of 12 oz. duck, with a floor of 8 oz. duck which snaps into rings all around the bottom of the tent walls. Underneath this canvas floor we will first lay two strips of light

Editor's Note—This is a newly discovered non-fiction work by ERB, which ran in the author's local community paper, *Oak Leaves* (Oak Park, Illinois), April 29, 1916.

weight linoleum to keep out all ground dampness, and inside the tent the canvas floor will be covered by Navajo rugs.

Two of the rooms will be used as sleeping apartments by Mrs. Burroughs, our three children and the nurse maid. The third room will be a combination kitchen and dining room, as well as a rainy-day living room.

The tent has two doors and two windows. The latter will be screened with ordinary cloth netting, while the former will have detachable wire screen doors and frames, which may be securely locked upon the inside. This is a concession to Mrs. Burroughs' recollection of a former day when we lived in an ordinary "A" tent in the Sawtooth Mountains of Idaho, when horse flies as large as milk bottles infested the tent by day and ground squirrels made life hideous by night in their unholy attempts to drag hams and sides of bacon from their hiding places near our cots, while the dense pine woods, upon every hand gave forth weird sounds that could have been—and were—attributed to the silver-tips that were known to lair there.

Five folding camp beds will accommodate, m or 1 uncomfortably, the occupants of the tent. The chauffeur and I will sleep outside—he at one end of the tent, and I at the other, as a further precaution against the lions, tigers and garter snakes which are known to infest the unexplored wildernesses east of the Alleghenies.

There will be canvas covers for packing and roping each bed while on the march, folding camp chairs, folding tables, a good size ice chest, a kerosene cook stove, a fireless cooker, twenty-seven miles of mosquito netting, kitchen utensils and all the thousand and one things which will be necessary to make the family comfortable in camp and the chauffeur and me swear while making or breaking camp.

There will also be two American flags and 1 doz. 22E902 asbestos lighting rings that I am earnestly advised by the catalog to take along for use in the kerosene cook stove. The catalog doesn't tell me what they are for or how to use them. They constitute the one, or rather the one dozen things that are occasioning me the greatest anticipatory perturbation at present. Oh, yes, there is another thing that is not entirely clear to me. Possibly I can obtain value received from this letter if I solicit suggestions on the subject. I refer to the bath question.

I had thought of carrying along sufficient water in a specially constructed tank for several underdeveloped baths; but the only folding tubs I have found were too large and cumbersome. I also have worked out a more or less practical shower arrangement; but this would not answer for the children, since the water for their baths must be heated. Of course there is an alternative which makes for ease—that of bathing in June, just before leaving, and again in the fall after we return.

The transport will consist of two machines— a touring car that will carry the family and maid, which I shall drive (I refer to the car), and a light truck for the camp equipment. This will be in charge of the chauffeur. I have been trying to remember to call the thing a motor lorry—it sounds much more romantic even if it doesn't exactly describe it. I am in hopes that by so designating it I shall succeed in arousing its pride so that it will act like a motor lorry. It didn't the day I bought it— instead it ran a mile and a half of the eight miles home, after which I had to tow it the balance of the way. Since then we have been delving into its innermost secrets and buying new parts.

Our route is laid out. We shall go first to Coldwater Lake, Michigan, where we shall practice for a week or so, and then we shall take the best road east, keeping to the best roads until it is time to turn about and start west again. We shall camp where we find a favorable spot, making but a few miles a day, for we are going for pleasure and there is no pleasure in hurry. If we like a place sufficiently we shall remain several days, or several weeks, or all summer. We have no destination. Destinations are the bane of travel—especially automobile travel. They take away all the rest and comfort and pleasure of the journey—they clog the mind with worry and apprehension, for fear they won't be there when you arrive or that you won't arrive while they are there—and they hide the beauties of the wayside in a cloud of dust and a blur of speed.

We shall break no records, unless some one has previously hung up a record for procrastination, in which event we shall go out after it. We know pretty well how fast our car will go—something like seventy two or three miles an hour, I believe. I have already had it up to sixty, which is thirty miles an hour faster than anyone should drive—so I shall not mind if a constant stream of one cylinder Buicks and Model T's are passing us by day and by night. We are going to wear khaki and shall not mind the dust.

Then, if we went over twenty miles an hour we should probably lose the motor lorry, which, after all, may be the real reason for taking our time. One doesn't flee at seventy-three miles an hour away from a well stocked refrigerator travelling at twenty.

I see that I have neglected mention of one of the important members of the expedition. He is a son of Bogey. Many of you know Bogey. She belongs to Dick Salter and has had a club on Marion Street named for her. Bogey is some dog; but she cannot approximate her young son, Tarzan. He is to be *askari* of the safari.

I have promised Mr. McFeely that when we are en route I will send a photograph to *Oak Leaves* showing an intimate picture of the horrors of roughing de luxe.

· · · · ·

In all the literature of mankind, only Sherlock Holmes
is nearly as well known as Tarzan. This popularity is justified.
Tarzan of the Apes *is a great and fabulous adventure epic. . . .it*
seems likely that at least Tarzan will be printed and read long after
many authors "with pointed messages for our times"
have been forgotten.
—Sam Moskowitz

EDGAR RICE BURROUGHS

Man or Tumblebug

Appeal for Suburban Reserve Battalion—Author of
"Tarzan of the Apes" Says a Few Things

There was a paragraph in B.L.T.'s column a few days ago that seemed to me to typify American patriotism a little better than anything I have yet seen.

"My only regret is that I have but one mouth to shoot off for my country."

We are demons for patriotism when the sacrifice entailed embraces such heroic actions as rising to the strains of "The Star Spangled Banner," uncovering to the flag and explaining to the missus how it should have been done and would have if we had been in Wilson's place. I am not speaking now of the men who have already enlisted in the navy, the army, the National Guard or the reserve officers' training camps. They have attained by their deeds a pinnacle of patriotism to which no amount of conversation may ever elevate us. Nor am I speaking of you alone—I am speaking of us both; of every able bodied man who is not enrolled in some military activity at this moment.

Oh, yes, I know we have good excuses; but which of us clamors to occupy a position which requires excuses? I don't. As a matter of fact there is no excuse. The question is did you go, or did you not, when your country called? For my part I shall make no excuses; but never again shall I rise to the national anthem or uncover to my country's flag without an inward sense of shame until I can do so clothed in the uniform of some branch of national defense, however humble.

We are all of us eager to insist that we have the will to do. Well, then, let us do something! We have the opportunity now to prove that we are willing to shoot off something beside our months for our country, and that opportunity comes to us under the title of "The Oak Park Reserve Battalion," which is being recruited from men of all ages who are physically fit to endure two hours drill a week.

The purposes of the organization are, briefly, to fit men for the eventuality which may face us all in consequence of a protracted war with Germany, of the withdrawal of our state troops for federal service or of internal disturbances which, in the light of all history, are foregone conclusions at such a time as this. The requirements and sacrifices are negligible—they should be greater, for no man who is fit to live in a community of men but should welcome the opportunity for sacrifice if only that he may set an example to those who shall come after us.

There has been one meeting, at which every eligible man present, I should

Editor's Note—This is a newly discovered non-fiction work by ERB, which ran in the author's local community paper, *Oak Leaves* (Oak Park, Illinois), May 26, 1917.

judge, volunteered his services. There will be another meeting in the council room of the Municipal building before *Oak Leaves* goes to press. If you did not attend either of these meetings call up the defense committee, Oak Park 6300, and ask when the next meeting will be held and where. Get into this. Don't wait to be dragged in, or coaxed in, or shamed in. Go in of your own volition. If you haven't heard of this movement before, it is not your fault that you are not in now; but after today it is your fault if you don't make an effort of your own to enlist in the reserve battalion.

There are personal advantages to be derived from membership; but I do not believe that they should ever be discussed. There are some things which are so sacred, so holy that a man should shrink from the thought of profiting from them. The man who links duty with dividends would doubly congratulate himself upon his wife's virtue because of the high cost of divorce proceedings.

To the wives and mothers who read this I appeal for assistance. Ask your husbands and your sons to read it. Urge them to join. There is about one chance in a million that this unit ever will see service of any nature; but it is against that one chance that we are organizing—this is true preparedness; and if the one chance comes you do not want other women's sons and husbands to protect you and your home and your husband.

To the clergy of Oak Park and River Forest I appeal for assistance. You can do much from your pulpits tomorrow and next Sunday and the Sunday thereafter to awaken the men of your congregations to a sense of their duty. You can advocate Sunday drill for those who have no other time to train themselves to protect their churches and their homes. A German invasion is remote; but not impossible. Military experts have proven this. You know what Germans have done to the churches of Belgium and France. You know that to the German mind there is but one God and he is a German god and his representative on earth is the Kaiser. Let us drill on Sundays, then, to protect our God from the German god, and while we drill, our women can pray—pray that we be made fit to deserve any God at all.

On the rifle range at Fort Grant, Arizona, we used to lie in the sun and watch the tumblebugs while awaiting our turns to miss the target. Are you familiar with the ways of the tumblebug? He stands on his head and rolls a little ball of dung backward with his hind legs. He can't see where he is going and he has but a single thought in his head—that is his ball of dung and he wants to bury it in his own hole in the ground. You may annihilate fellow tumblebugs all about him; but he does not rush to their rescue—he just keeps on rolling his own little ball. Sometimes another tumblebug comes and pretends to help him, but the second tumblebug's designs are only sinister. If he gets a chance he swipes the ball. The tumblebug is the epitome of selfishness and moral blindness.

Are you a man, or are you a tumblebug? The answer will be found in the roster of the Oak Park reserve battalion.

· · · · ·

EDGAR RICE BURROUGHS

Arms and the Woman

I am about to record a sad fact—sorrowfully and with tears in my eyes, because I know that after it is recorded I may have to leave town to escape the mussiness of being thrown out. I heave a heartfelt sigh and proclaim: The greatest obstacle the Reserve Battalion has had to meet is woman—lovely woman! Or rather that sub-species of the divine sex vulgarly known as "friend wife." I now adjust my gas-mask and steel helmet and don my asbestos shoes against the liquid fire of a counter-attack. I expect to be overwhelmed by a barrage of petticoats.

There are exceptions. I therefore except the exceptions. Being a devotee of the safety first idea, I pause to chronicle that my own wife has encouraged me in the work of the Reserve Battalion. She not only permits me to go out as many evenings a week as possible, but encourages me to do so. Which gives me pause, wherein I scratch my head and reminisce upon my former popularity.

Ask any married man in the battalion for the hoariest joke of the organization and he will tell you of the wife who threatens to sue for divorce on the grounds of desertion—because her husband is out two or three nights a week. A sad commentary on the active loyalty of our women. They are all loyal, God bless 'em! if it doesn't interfere with their convenience.

Do you know what the trouble is? They do not yet realize that we are at war. They do not realize that Germany has already thrashed Belgium and Servia and Roumania and Russia and Italy, and that so far not one of the central powers has been thrashed. They do not know that the chances are more than equal that we shall be left "holding the bag" after all of Europe has been defeated. The war is not won. As far as we are concerned it has not started. We have before us all of our pain and grief and sacrifices and sorrows, and yet there are wives here who would rather take their husbands to a card party at the Colonial, or dance until 2 o'clock in the morning, than to sacrifice these pleasures that their men may fit themselves for the inevitable; for, as sure as God is God, the time is coming when every he-man in America shall be called upon to fight.

The work of the Reserve Battalion is a little thing—I grant you that. We are infinitesimal electrons in the great world-mass that is struggling for the supremacy of right over wrong; but the mass is as the electrons are. If the electrons are weak and vascillating, the mass will be weak and vascillating. We must see to it that our part of the work is done with the strength of men—of strong men—and the sacrificing devotion of strong women.

Editor's Note—This is a newly discovered non-fiction work by ERB, which ran in the author's local community paper, *Oak Leaves* (Oak Park, Illinois), November 3, 1917.

If I were guiding the destinies of a social club in Oak Park or River Forest I should see to it that card parties and dances were held at such times as would not interfere with the work of the men of the Reserve Battalion. I should almost be willing to curtail dances and card parties in the realization that neither one nor the other was in harmony with the spirit of the times, nor ever in the history of the world did either win a war.

Do you know that the banks are warning us that one-half the income of every American is to be needed for the winning of this war? Think of it! ONE-HALF YOUR INCOME! Can you not give up one-half your leisure?—one-half your pleasures?

Many of you have seen the Reserve Battalion parades and reviews. How many of you have seen the serious work that these men are doing? How many of you realize that company drills are held once and twice a week for every company, in addition to the Sunday morning drill? How many of you know of the non-commissioned officers' schools that are held nightly in the municipal building and the high school?

How many of you guess at the time and money that are being put into this work by loyal citizens of Oak Park and River Forest? Can you place your pleasure and your transient entertainment against the serious work of earnest men? Can you dance and play bridge at the expense of a really necessary endeavor, and enjoy it? Very well, I couldn't.

While other women's husbands are in France, can you begrudge two or three nights a week for the training of your husband in the protection of his home against the unseen forces of the Kaiser, such as overthrew Russia, and against the great chance that France and England may fail as have Russia and Italy, leaving us at the mercy of the Hun?

Wherewith I retire to my bombproof.

• • • • •

I can remember as a child reading with breathless fascination
the Mars novels of Edgar Rice Burroughs. I journeyed with John Carter,
gentleman adventurer from Virginia, to "Barsoom,". . . . I followed herds of
eight legged beasts of burden, the thoats. I won the hand of the lovely Dejah
Thoris, Princess of Helium. I befriended a four-metre-high green fighting man
named Tars Tarkas. . . . Might it really be possible—in fact and not in fancy—
to venture with John Carter to the Kingdom of Helium on the planet Mars? . . .
I can remember spending many an hour in my boyhood, arms resolutely
outstretched in an empty field, imploring what I believed to be
Mars to transport me there.

—*Carl Sagan*

124

Go To Pershing

The war may be over, and then again, it may not; but whether it is or no there are still battles to be fought. In the brief span of eighteen months we have arisen from indolence and fat sloth to become one of the foremost fighting nations of the world. That was a battle in itself—a great battle of brains and efficiency and energy against ignorance, indifference and laziness.

Today we are the greatest nation on earth and today we must again throw down the gage of battle to ignorance, indifference and laziness if we are to remain the greatest nation on earth.

And how shall we prepare to fight this battle? The war has taught us much. It has taught us how efficiency and energy may be attained—how brains may be quickened and developed. It has shown us what military training can do for men.

Each of us has seen and remarked upon the almost miraculous changes wrought in friends and acquaintances by a few weeks of intensive training. We have seen the flippant, the indifferent, the indolent, transformed into keen, alert, serious minded men, imbued with a full appreciation of their responsibilities and a pride in achievement such as it would have been beyond their capacities to experience formerly.

The need for training fighting men to bear the weapons of destruction may be over—let us hope and pray that it is over. But we must still train fighting men—fighting men to bear the implements of construction and reconstruction. And we must train them in the same way—the way that we have found to be the best way to train fighting men, whether for war or for peace—by intensive military training.

We are going to continue the civilian training camps such as became famous through Plattsburgh, Sheridan and Steever. These camps have become almost a part of our national life. They will continue and they will grow. Every section of the country, every season of the year will see them. Already their graduates are scattered from coast to coast and wherever you find one you will find a high type of citizen intelligently enthusiastic concerning the value of military training to the men in civil life.

The next great camp is to be held in the Zachary Taylor cantonment in Lou-

Editor's Note—An attempt is made in Jerry L. Schneider's *Edgar Rice Burroughs Tells All* (Pulpville Press, 3rd edition, 2008), to compile all of ERB's non-fiction work, however this article is not included. It is listed as a "Known Unpublished Work." Nevertheless, "Go To Pershing" was published in at least one newspaper, as we uncovered its appearance in the *Logansport Daily Tribune* (Logansport, Indiana) for December 27, 1918.

isville, Ky. commencing January 6th. It will be known as Camp Pershing. Indications point toward its being the greatest camp of its kind ever held. The last two camps at Steever were over-enrolled—applications had to be rejected. Camp Pershing will be over-enrolled to an even greater extent if the last two camps at Steever are any criterion and I think they are.

If you have never attended one of these camps, I, who have, can give you some inside information. In the first place, let me tell you that time will not hang heavily upon your hands—you will find that from reveille to taps there will be something doing ever minute. Setting up exercises started the day at Steever—and you'll find that you need them—muscles and joints have become rusty from disuse. Pretty soon they'll atrophy or ossify and you'll be an old man, unless Camp Pershing gives them a new lease on life.

Those setting-up exercises were hard at first—on some of us. I recall one in particular. It is called the jumping-jack. The first morning I leaped blithely. The second morning I was still blithe, but I did not leap so high. The third morning I could not get my feet off the ground—all I could do was wave my arm; but before the end of the camp I could have jumped over a cow—a small cow.

Then, there was the swim! Oh, boy, but maybe that wasn't joy! And maybe you didn't feel fit for mess that followed. After mess came inspection and then drill, followed possibly by a lecture, and then more drill. The drills were interesting and snappy, bringing back to your old blood the fire of youth.

We swam again after the last morning drill period and then ate. And so it went through the balance of the day, with retreat parade after supper. We sang a lot and composed strange and wonderful company yells and generally acted like kids, for we had a mighty good time sandwiched in with all the hard work.

And we made friends. That is one of the finest things about these camps—the making of new friendships between men from different sections of our country. They are going to help to weld the business interests of the nation, for in these camps you meet the highest types from the commercial and professional ranks of society.

The best meets the best, for the very excellent reason that the broadest and most intelligence men are the first to appreciate the value to be derived from this sort of training. It is they who fill the camps to overflowing.

And what does it do for you? Of course it improves your health and makes you feel fit and strong and you have a good time while you are at camp; but these are not, desirable as they are, the greatest ultimate benefits that you derive, nor either is the fact that you will have laid the foundation of military knowledge that may some day, and soon, permit you to serve your state or your country in a military capacity.

Military training makes you a better and broader man. It makes you more efficient. It will prolong your life while it makes that life more useful to society and more agreeable to yourself. It quickens your mind—you will find that you meet and grasp the problems of your business life more efficiently after military training than before it.

Capt. Edgar Rice Burroughs,
Illinois Reserve Militia,
Oak Park, Illinois, 1918.

It inculcates habits of self-discipline and self-control and there is no need for expatiating on the value of these two characteristics to an audience of businessmen. It teaches tact and resourcefulness and, possibly greatest of all for large employers, it demonstrates the proper methods of handling large bodies of men.

A case in point: A boy of twenty commanded the company of one hundred and nineteen men in which I chanced to serve at Steever. He was our instructor. Most of us were old enough to have been his father and many might have been his grandfather insofar as difference in age was concerned. There were many businessmen in the company. One of them owned a chain of restaurants in Omaha and employed hundreds of people. Another was the head of a large railroad system and there were enough militia majors to have taken Berlin; but I venture to say that there was not one who did not learn something from that boy about handling men, and some of us learned a lot.

Training camps should become a life habit of every man over thirty. He should invest two weeks of every year of his life in a training camp and he should consider it a necessary investment that he owes to himself and his wife and his family and society, just as he considers life insurance such an investment. It is a mighty good investment that will pay dividends in real money, in real health, in real happiness and in longevity.

When I read an article of this kind by a professional writer, I often say to myself: "I wonder if this guy knows what he's talking about." Because I am so sincere and earnest in my belief in the value of military training and so anxious that every man who reads this article shall consider it seriously as applying to himself I want to tell you something. I have been preaching for a long time the value of military training to men of all ages and in this article I state that it is of value to both business and professional men. I started my first military training at the age of sixteen; I trained again at the age of forty-three. I was a businessman until I was thirty-five and since then I have been a professional man. So I think I know what I am talking about.

Take my advice— Go to Camp Pershing!

Syndicated ERB Newspaper Art

The popularity of Burroughs' stories quickly led to their syndication in the newspaper market during the mid-Teens. It was common for a newspaper syndicate to commission new art to accompanying its serialized novels. J. Allen St. John himself illustrated an edition of *Tarzan and the Jewels of Opar* for the *Chicago Herald* in 1915.

Subjective to the space available, papers did not always run every piece of art with each installment, making the task of locating an entire series of art for any given novel very difficult.

What follows is a selection of some of this rarely seen art, pulled from newspaper and microfilm archives. Please excuse the extreme variance in quality.

Story header

Chapter I.

With Mighty Blows of His Open Palms
He Felled One After Another.

"Is She Not Both Young and Good Looking?" Asked Kovudoo.

The Son of Tarzan, Chapter IX.

He Wound His Trunk About the Ape Man's Body.

The Son of Tarzan, Chapter X.

But at the Flash of the Explosion He Stopped.

The Son of Tarzan, Chapter IX.

*The Author of That Strange Story "Tarzan of the Apes"
Has Written an Even Stranger Romance Entitled*

The Gods of Mars

H. G. Wells and Jules Verne Outdone ❖ ❖ ❖ ❖ ❖
Read About the Plant Men, the Green Men and the Black Pirates of Mysterious Barsoom ❖ ❖ ❖ ❖ ❖

One of the Big Six Serials

Read of John Carter's Valiant Efforts to Rescue Dejah Thoris, His Beautiful Princess, From the Valley Dor and the Temples of Issus ❖ ❖ ❖ ❖ ❖

*Do Not Miss
Our New Serial* THE GODS of MARS

It will begin in The Daily Free Press tomorrow

The Daily Free Press, (Carbondale, Illinois) January 24, 1917

Editor's note: What follows is believed to be the complete set of illustrations for this novel.

Story header

"Goodby, nephew," he said. "I may
never see you again."

Its Hairless Body Was of a Strange and
Ghoulish Blue.

Chapter I.

Foreword

"The Gods of Mars" By EDGAR RICE BURROUGHS,

Author of "Tarzan of the Apes," "The Return of Tarzan,"
"The Eternal Lover," Etc.

*If you follow John Carter to Mars in the first few paragraphs of this story
you will follow him clean through to the end of his adventures on the red planet.
Imagination and literary ability gave Edgar Rice Burroughs the power to write
this story of the terrible plant-men and the Black Pirates of Barsoom and
Issus, frightful goddess of the First Born—just as they gave birth in his brain
to wonderful "Tarzan of the Apes."*

The Green Warrior Was Much Put to
It to Hold His Own.

Chapter II.

We Strained and Struggled About the
Tree.

Chapter III.

Ventured Out Upon the Limb, Then
Beat a Hasty Retreat.

Chapter III.

Instantly I Sprang Toward It to Wrench
It Open Again.

Chapter IV.

"This, John Carter, is—heaven."

Chapter IV.

It Did Not Take Me Long to Fall Easily Into My Fighting Stride.

Chapter V.

"Release me, and I will give you entrance to the other horror chamber."

Chapter V.

Chapter VI.

I Looked to See Her Torn to Pieces.

The Girl Raised Her Revolver and Fired Point Blank at Him.

Chapter VI.

A Continuous Line of Impregnable Fortifications Circles the Outer Slopes.

Chapter VII.

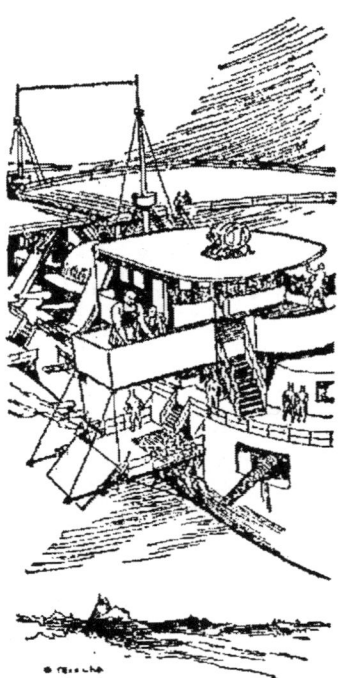

With Headlong Speed We Rushed Away From the Terrible Scenes.

On, Steadily on, Came the Grim Black Craft.

Chapter VIII.

Chapter VIII.

With Drawn Swords They Made For
Me.

Chapter IX.

He Flung His Sword Upon the Ground
Before Me.

Chapter IX.

"Seize him!" cried Zat Arras.

Chapter X.

"Hold! Let no man move till I am
done."

Chapter XI.

"Death!" shouted one of the judges.

Chapter XI.

One of the Blacks Tore Her Dagger From Her.

Chapter XII.

I Took a Solemn Vow to Reach, Rescue and Revenge My Princess.

Chapter XIII.

Nothing Shall Stay Me Now Short of Death.

Chapter XIII.

"A thern!" whispered Tars Tarkas.

Chapter XIII.

"A great fleet of battleships south-southeast, my prince!" he cried.

Chapter XIII.

Now the Two Great Fleets Closed in a Titanic Struggle.

Chapter XIV.

"You are my prisoner, Zat Arras!" cried.

Chapter XIV.

"Help, John Carter! We are suffocating!"

Chapter XV.

"Where Is Dejah Thoris?"

Chapter XVI.

When She Saw Me She Rushed Toward the Bars That Separated Us.

Chapter XVI.

"I shall not leave you, then, my princess," I replied.

Chapter XVI.

10¢ PER COPY

November, 1927

The JOURNAL HOUSEHOLD

The GIRL from Hollywood

by Edgar Rice Burroughs

¶ "Women are cheaper in Hollywood than in any town this side of Port Said," said a motion-picture director not long ago. And he was not thinking of them as economic factors.

¶ "Not one in a hundred has a chance; but they see only the big money and the luxurious life of a 'star'! and so they go on, 'waiting' for a 'chance'. And to get it——? Well, ask any casting director. If he gives you an honest answer, you'll blush."

CHAPTER I.

THE TWO HORSES picked their way carefully downward over the loose shale of the steep hillside. The big bay stallion in the lead sidled mincingly, tossing his head nervously, and flecking the flannel shirt of his rider with foam. Behind the man on the stallion a girl rode a clean-limbed bay of lighter color, whose method of descent, while less showy, was safer, for he came more slowly, and in the very bad places he braced his four feet forward and slid down, sometimes almost sitting upon the ground.

At the base of the hill there was a narrow level strip; then an eight-foot wash, with steep banks, barred the way to the opposite side of the canon, which rose gently to the hills beyond. At the foot of the descent the man reined in and waited until the girl was safely down; then he wheeled his mount and trotted toward the wash. Twenty feet from it he gave the animal its head and a word. The horse broke into a gallop, took off at the edge of the wash, and cleared it so effortlessly as almost to give the impression of flying.

Behind the man came the girl, but her horse came at the wash with a rush—not the slow, steady gallop of the stallion—and at the very brink he stopped to gather himself. The dry bank caved beneath his front feet, and into the wash he went, head first.

The man turned and spurred back. The girl looked up from her saddle, making a wry face.

"No damage?" he asked, an expression of concern upon his face.

"No damage," the girl replied. "Senator is clumsy enough at jumping, but no matter what happens he always lights on his feet."

(Continued on page 3)

"Of course I'll marry you—some day; but not yet. Why, I haven't lived yet, Custer!"

Early and rare reprint appearance of *The Girl from Hollywood*.

 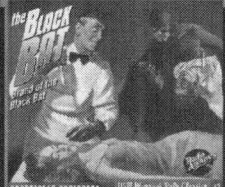  
   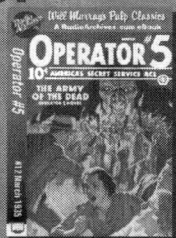 
    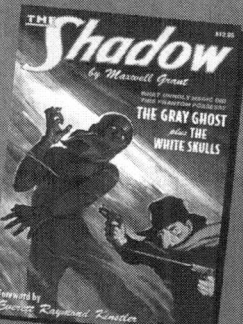

Select ERB Book Reviews

Most of the novels of Edgar Rice Burroughs received wide-spread publicity campaigns, with many of those books receiving reviews in major newspapers. Here is a brief selection of some of those reviews.

TARZAN OF THE APES. By Edgar Rice Burroughs. (A. C. McClurg & Co. $1.30.) The author has evidently tried to see how far he could go without exceeding the limits of possibility. Lord Greystoke and his wife are marooned on the African jungle coast, build a cabin, and become accustomed to the wild life there. A son is born and the mother dies. A herd of giant apes invade the cabin, kill Lord Greystoke, take away the child, and rear it as their own. When the child has become a man he possesses the habits, the language, and the great strength of the apes. One day a white woman is put ashore from a ship, and the ape man falls in love with her, and rescues her from many perils. He also plays the part of instructor to a scientific expedition. The scene then shifts to Wisconsin, where the heroine is rescued from more perils. Meanwhile the ape man has been educated in the culture of his kind, and he finally proves that he has a soul as well as superhuman strength.

Tarzan of the Apes
The New York Times
June 11, 1914

BURROUGHS' LATEST HIS MOST FANTASTIC YARN

'The Chessmen of Mars," by Edgar Rice Burroughs — Another in Mr Burroughs' fantastic series of Martian yarns, it but further proves the marvelous qualities of his imagination and his clever descriptive powers. The tale is mainly concerned with the romance and adventures of a princess of Helium who being lost, is captured by hostile and strange beings. Surely no other writer ever conceived of such a race as Mr Burroughs tells of or of adventures such as happened to the Princess and her champions before she was delivered from her captors. The weird story is written in the masterly manner of this clever author and there is not a page in it that is not of arresting interest. Chicago: A. C. McClurg & Co.

The Chessmen of Mars
The Boston Globe
December 16, 1922

"THE MUCKER"

" The Mucker," by Edgar Rice Burroughs (Chicago: A. C. McClurg & Co.), is a wildly improbable tale that rushes through the tough section of Chicago, California, Honolulu, an unfrequented Japanese Island where Japs in medieval armor dwell, New York, Kansas and Mexico in the days of Villa. There is bloodshed galore, wild rides and battle against all sorts of dangers. The hero, who starts as a callous mucker, is shaped in the hard school of danger and the soft school of love into a decent man. Mr. Burroughs, who is responsible for the Tarzan yarns, proves that he has a fertile imagination and small respect for probabilities.

The Mucker,
The New York Times
November 27, 1921

142

LOST ON VENUS
By Edgar Rice Burroughs
Edgar Rice Burroughs Inc., Pub.

Whether you are a "Tarzan" fan or not, and notwithstanding the fact that you possibly don't care for the average fantastic fairy tale type of story, you can't help but like "Lost on Venus." There is a lot of comedy in the adventures of Carson Napier in his adventures on the far off planet Venus where he falls in love with Duane, daughter of the king of that country.

Carson and Duane jump from one devastating adventure into another so quickly, that by the time you have remembered the name and kind of one of the queer Venusian animals which have attacked them, they have thwarted them and encountered others.

Imagine being shut in a room with seven doors, each doorway open to a passageway of horror—poison gases, closing walls and an infuriated carnivorous tharban, combination of lion and porcupine, of a passageway of corrosive acids which eat into the flesh, etc. That was the first adventure of Carson Napier on Venus.

Later, he has hand to hand battles with such fiendish beings as hair covered cannibals, a group of bastos (head similar to an American Bison, curved tusks, horrible beasts) the vere (a hideous lizard like animal twenty feet in length) and many other such evil things, not to mention a race of dead and bloodless people who have been trained by a leader Skor, who only sought living persons to experiment on them, taking their blood for tests in regard to keeping corpses under his thumb.

The story is amusing and entertaining and certainly not unmoral.

Lost On Venus
Daily-Journal World
(Lawrence, Kansas)
July 6, 1935

THE OAKDALE and THE RIDER
by Edgar Rice Burroughs
Edgar Rice Burroughs, Inc., Tarzana, Calif., Publishers

The two Burroughs' novels incorporated in this volume are adventure stories laid in widely separated locales.

THE OAKDALE AFFAIR is the story of a lovable vagabond and a pseudo badman, whose trials and adventures are not unmixed with comedy as well as stark tragedy culminating in a lynching party.

If you like mystery and red-blooded adventure, you will enjoy this story of the open-road on a stormy night, of hoboes, and murderers, and a haunted house.

THE RIDER takes you into the mountainous wilds of mythical Balkan kingdoms where cross the paths of a dare-devil crown prince, a notorious highwayman, an American heiress, a Balkan princess, and an adventurous American.

In both stories are mystery, thrilling situations, and last, but not least, love.

The Oakdale Affair and The Rider
Meriden Record
(Meriden, Connecticut)
March 11, 1937

The Girl from Hollywood: By Edgar Rice Burroughs. The Macauley Company, New York. Mr. Burroughs won a vogue thru his impossible Tarzan stories, and should have stuck to the forests. Changing his scene to California, and giving as his excuse for writing this story that "Woman are cheaper there than in any town this side of Port Said." he lets us know what to expect right at the start. The crude methods that made his Ape-Man acceptable do not fit his new theme, and the story might better not have been written.

The Girl From Hollywood
The Davenport Democrat and Leader
(Davenport, Iowa)
September 23, 1923

Edgar R. Burroughs, Who Made Millions On Tarzan, Is Dead

Tarzana, Calif. (UP) — Edgar Rice Burroughs, creator of modern fiction's fabulous Tarzan the Apeman, died quietly while reading in bed Sunday.

The 74-year-old author made Tarzan an international legend which earned him millions of dollars. The jungle hero's tree-swinging antics were known to millions everywhere and only the Bible exceeded Tarzan stories in sales.

Mr. Burroughs, a shut-in for the last few years, was reading the Sunday comics at he ate breakfast in bed. Suddenly the newspaper dropped from his hands. His eyes closed. And the famed novelist died almost instantly.

Dr. Herman Seal, the writer's personal physician, was in the ranchhouse when Mr. Burroughs died. He said death was caused by a heart ailment and hardening of the arteries. Mr. Burroughs had been critically ill for the last 10 days.

Also present were his three children, Mrs. Joan Pierce, Hulbert and John Burroughs.

Mr. Burroughs once explained in brief terms why he created his fabulous jungle men who captured the fancy and imagination of the world: "I needed the money."

He was an unsuccesswul salesman for a pencil-sharpener manufacturer when he suddenly felt he could succeed as a writer.

"If people were paid for writing such rot," he said referring to pulp-magazine stores, "I figured I could write stuff just as bad."

"Tarzan of the Apes" was his first successful novel He wrote it originally as a serial with A. A. McClurg publishing it in book form.

After that, Tarzan was spread throughout the literate world by almost every conceivable means.

Twenty-six motion pictures were made from which Mr. Burroughs got about $5,000,000.

The apeman stories were translated in 56 languages and Mr. Burroughs boasted that not one of his more than 40 titles was ever out of print.

As a comic-strip, Tarzan achieved sucess similar to the author's novels and movie versions.

———————◆———————

The Evening News, (Tonawanda, NY) Monday, March 20, 1950, p.5

144

Press photo
circulated at the time
of Burroughs' death.

Author Buys Oak Park Home

Edgar Rice Burroughs, author of "Tarzan" and many other books now enjoying great popularity, has bought the residence at 700 Linden, owned and occupied by William H. Gardner, and will take posession on Monday. Mr. Burroughs and his family have lived in Oak Park for several years but a year ago began living the lives of gypsies, traveling across the continent in an automobile caravan, during which they had many adventures, pleasant and otherwise. Mr. Burroughs did a five-year bit in the regular army before the Spanish war.

Mr. and Mrs. Gardner will occupy the residence at Iowa and East.

Oak Leaves
(Oak Park, Illinois)
April 14, 1917

Index to advertisers

Made in the USA
Lexington, KY
12 February 2017